Samsung Galaxy S®

FOR

DUMMIES®

Samsung Galaxy S®
FOR
DUMMIES®

by Bill Hughes

WILEY

Wiley Publishing, Inc.

Samsung Galaxy S® For Dummies®

Published by
Wiley Publishing, Inc.
111 River Street
Hoboken, NJ 07030-5774

`www.wiley.com`

WILEY

About the Author

Bill Hughes is an experienced marketing strategy executive with over two decades of experience in sales, strategic marketing, and business development roles at several leading corporations, including Microsoft, IBM, General Electric, Motorola, and US West Cellular.

Recently, Bill has worked with Microsoft to enhance its marketing to mobile applications developers. He also has led initiatives to develop new products and solutions with several high-tech organizations, including Nextel, Motorola, SBC, and Tyco Electronics.

Bill has been a professor of marketing at the Kellogg School of Management at Northwestern University where he taught business marketing to graduate MBA students. In his lectures, he presented his findings on the validity of the market-research information used in financial analysis.

Bill also has written articles on this subject for several wireless industry trade magazines, as well as contributed to articles in *USA Today* and *Forbes*. These articles were based upon his research reports for In-Stat, where he was principal analyst, covering the wireless industry, specializing in smartphones and business applications of wireless devices. His most popular studies include "The Symbian Foundation: A Battle Royal for the Ecosystem," "Wireless Data in the Enterprise: The Hockey Stick Arrives," and "Cellphone Trends in the U.S. Enterprises: A Small Step from Personal Wireless."

He graduated with honors with an MBA degree from the Kellogg School of Management at Northwestern University and earned a bachelor of science degree with distinction from the College of Engineering at Cornell University, where he was elected to the Tau Beta Pi Engineering Honorary.

Bill lives in Bellevue, Washington, with his wife, Susan, and three sons, Ellis, Arlen, and Quinlan.

Dedication

I would like to dedicate this book to my late father, Robert J. Hughes, Sr.

Publisher's Acknowledgments

We're proud of this book; please send us your comments at http://dummies.custhelp.com. For other comments, please contact our Customer Care Department within the U.S. at 877-762-2974, outside the U.S. at 317-572-3993, or fax 317-572-4002.

Some of the people who helped bring this book to market include the following:

Acquisitions and Editorial

Project Editor: Rebecca Senninger

Acquisitions Editor: Katie Mohr

Senior Copy Editor: Teresa Artman

Technical Editors: Josh Mason, Kim Titus

Editorial Manager: Leah Cameron

Editorial Assistant: Amanda Graham

Sr. Editorial Assistant: Cherie Case

Cartoons: Rich Tennant
(www.the5thwave.com)

Composition Services

Project Coordinator: Patrick Redmond

Layout and Graphics: Claudia Bell, Samantha K. Cherolis, Cheryl Grubbs, Corrie Socolovitch, Erin Zeltner

Proofreaders: Rebecca Denoncour, Shannon Ramsey

Indexer: BIM Indexing & Proofreading Services

Publishing and Editorial for Technology Dummies

Richard Swadley, Vice President and Executive Group Publisher

Andy Cummings, Vice President and Publisher

Mary Bednarek, Executive Acquisitions Director

Mary C. Corder, Editorial Director

Publishing for Consumer Dummies

Diane Graves Steele, Vice President and Publisher

Composition Services

Debbie Stailey, Director of Composition Services

Contents at a Glance

Table of Contents

Introduction

· ·

*T*he Samsung Galaxy S is a powerful series of smartphones. As of the publication of this book, the Galaxy S series is the standard against which all other Android-based phones are measured.

I say "series" because each cellular carrier offers a slightly customized version of the Galaxy S line. Besides having a unique product name, Samsung incorporates special capabilities for each network to make each version slightly different.

The Galaxy S for AT&T is called Captivate and Vibrant for T-Mobile. Sprint offers the Epic 4G, and Verizon has the Fascinate. Although the phone name for each network is different, these phones are largely the same (at least one marketing person at each cellular carrier is cringing as you read this). This allows me to write this book covering the common capabilities.

Some of the differences between models are where hardware buttons are placed on the phone or the icons used to perform similar functions. In addition, some cellular carriers' Galaxy S versions come out of the box with preloaded applications, games, or files. Some come with accessories (like a corded headset), and others don't. I don't dwell on these kinds of differences.

At a more core level, these phones are built for high-speed wireless communications. The cellular carriers have spent kajillions upgrading their networks to offer more coverage and better data speeds than their competition. I don't spend time dwelling on these differences in network technology, either, because it doesn't really make much difference (again, at least one engineering person at each cellular carrier is cringing as you read this).

I assume that you already have a phone, and I just hope that you have good coverage where you spend more of your time with your phone. If so, you will be fine. If not, you need to switch to another network because the experience with your phone will be frustrating. Although it's not the fault of the phone, I hope that you can get out of your contract if you have poor coverage.

From this point on, I will point out only those differences among the Galaxy S phones that are otherwise relevant. Fortunately, all the Galaxy S phones offer you a similar experience. As long as you have good cellular data coverage, it will be an exciting experience!

The main thing to remember is that all Galaxy S phones use Google's Android platform. Think of how different brands of PCs are based upon Microsoft's Windows 7 operating system. Although there are some differences in how the OS appears when you turn on your PC for the first time, the experience is largely similar whether the PC comes from Dell or from HP (now there are at least two PC product managers, one at Dell and the other at HP, who are cringing). This is in contrast, say, to the experience when you bring up a PC running Ubuntu Linux, which is noticeably different.

The good news is that the Android platform has proven to be widely popular, even more successful than Google originally expected when it was first announced in November of 2007. More people are using Android-based phones of all manufacturers, and more third parties are writing applications. This is good news as this offers you more options for applications.

In addition, all Galaxy S phones use a powerful graphics processor from PowerVR, employ Samsung's super-bright Super AMOLED touchscreen, and are covered in Gorilla Glass. The superior screen experience differentiates this product line from other Android phones. Because of these enhanced capabilities, you can navigate around the screen with multi-touch screens instead of hierarchical menus that are found on lesser Android phones. Plus, videos look stunning from many angles.

Smartphones are getting smarter all the time, and the Galaxy S is one of the smartest. However, just because you've used a smartphone in the past doesn't mean you should expect to use your new Galaxy S without a bit of guidance.

You might not be familiar with using a multi-touch screen, plus there are lots of capabilities that you might not be familiar with. It would be unfortunate to find out from a kid in the neighborhood that the phone you have been carrying around for several months could solve a problem you have been having because you were never told that the solution was in your pocket the whole time.

In fact, Samsung is proud of the "usability" of its Galaxy S. Its user manual is really just a "quickstart" guide, and you can find additional instructions online. However, you have to know what you don't know to get what you want unless you plan to view every tutorial. And that's where this book comes in: your hands-on guide to getting the most from your Galaxy S.

About This Book

This book is a reference. You don't have to read it from beginning to end to get all you need out of it. The information is clearly organized and easy to access. And you don't need thick glasses to understand this book. This book helps you figure out what you want to do — and then tells you how to do it, in plain English.

Conventions Used in This Book

I don't use many conventions in this book, but there are a few you should know about:

- Whenever I introduce a new term, I put it in *italics* and define it shortly thereafter (often in parentheses).

- I use **bold** for the action parts of numbered steps, so you can easily see what you're supposed to do.

- I use `monofont` for Web addresses and e-mail addresses, so they stand out from the surrounding text. ***Note:*** When this book was printed, some Web addresses may have needed to break across two lines of text. If that happened, rest assured that we haven't put in any extra characters (such as hyphens) to indicate the break. So, when using one of these Web addresses, just type exactly what you see in this book, pretending as though the line break doesn't exist.

- I call the phone the "Galaxy S" unless I am referring to a particular version that is associated with a cellular carrier. If that's the case, I call it by its respective brand name, such as the Captivate for AT&T.

What You're Not to Read

I think you'll find every last word of this book scintillating, but I might be a little biased. The truth is that you don't have to read the following:

- **Sidebars:** Sidebars are those gray boxes throughout the book. They're interesting but not essential to the topic at hand, so if you're short on time or you want only the information you absolutely need, you can skip them.

- **Text marked with the Technical Stuff icon:** For more on this icon, see the "Icons Used in This Book" section, later in this Introduction.

Foolish Assumptions

You know what they say about assuming, so I don't do much of it in this book. But I do make a few assumptions about you:

- **You have a Galaxy S phone.** You might be thinking about buying a Galaxy S phone, but my money's on your already owning one. After all, getting your hands on the phone is the best part!

 ✓ **You're not totally new to cellphones.** You know that your Galaxy S phone is capable of doing more than the average cellphone, and you're eager to find out what your phone can do.

 ✓ **You've used a computer.** You don't have to be a computer expert, but you at least know how to check your e-mail and surf the Web.

How This Book Is Organized

The 18 chapters in this book are divided into six parts. Here's what you can find in each part.

Part 1: Getting Started

The first part of this book gets you familiar with the basic capabilities of your Galaxy S phone. Chapter 1 is an overview of all the great features that come with your Samsung Galaxy phone. Chapter 2 is an introduction to everything from turning it on and off, to managing battery life, and making your phone secure.

Part II: Communication

In Chapters 3 and 4, I cover the basics of placing and taking calls and sending texts. In Chapter 5, you find out how to add contacts so you don't have to always dial an entire phone number. Chapter 6 shows you how to use your smartphone to send e-mail. On your phone, you can manage the e-mail that is on your PC as well as view updates from your friends within a given social network site. This adds a new level of convenience for staying in touch with friends while you're on the go.

Part III: Live on the Internet: Going Mobile

In Chapter 7, I show you how to access the Internet from your Galaxy S phone. Chapter 8 introduces you to the widgets and applications that come on your phone. I also introduce you to the Android Market in Chapter 9, where you can trick out your phone with more apps.

Part IV: Entertainment Applications

In this part, I cover the multimedia capabilities — music and video — of the Galaxy S phone (Chapter 13). The Galaxy S phone also allows you to play games (Chapter 11) and take snazzy photos (Chapter 10).

Part V: Productivity Applications

In this part, I look at the many ways you can use your phone for business. You can manage your work calendar (Chapter 14) and work on Microsoft office files on your Galaxy S phone (Chapter 15).

Part VI: The Part of Tens

This wouldn't be a *For Dummies* book without The Part of Tens. This part covers ten ways to customize the phone to make it truly your own and ten capabilities to look for in future releases.

Icons Used in This Book

Throughout this book, I use *icons* (little pictures in the margin) to draw your attention to various types of information. Here's a key to what those icons mean:

This whole book is like one series of tips. When I share especially useful tips and tricks, I mark it with the Tip icon.

This book is a reference, which means you don't have to commit it to memory — there is no test at the end. But once in a while, I do tell you things that are so important that I think you should remember them, and when I do, I mark them with the Remember icon.

Whenever you may do something that could cause a major headache, I warn you with the, er, Warning icon.

Whenever I start veering into technical territory, I slap a big ol' Technical Stuff icon on it. If you're a geek (or just like reading every single word), you'll find these icons interesting. If not, you aren't missing anything critical.

Part I
Getting Started

The 5th Wave — By Rich Tennant

ORICHTENNANT

Cell Phone

"This model comes with a particularly useful function — a simulated static button for breaking out of long-winded conversations."

In this part . . .

Your Samsung Galaxy S can be lots of fun and can make you very productive . . . but only if you know how to use it. Whether this is your first time using a smartphone or your first time using a touch screen, the chapters in this part give you the information you need to get started.

Exploring What You Can Do

Whether you want just the basics from a phone (make and take phone calls, customize your ringtone, take some pictures, maybe use a Bluetooth headset) or you want your phone to be always by your side (a tool for multiple uses all throughout your day), you can make that happen. In this chapter, I outline all the things your phone can do — from the basics, to what makes Galaxy S phones different from the rest. Throughout the remainder of the book, I walk you through the steps you need to take to get your phone doing what makes you the happiest.

Discovering the Basics of Your Phone

All cellphones on the market today include basic functions, and even some entry-level phones are a little more sophisticated. Of course, Samsung includes all basic functions on the Galaxy S model. In addition to making and taking calls (see Chapter 3) and sending and receiving texts (see Chapter 4), the Galaxy S sports the following basic features:

- ✓ **5MP digital camera:** This resolution is more than enough for posting good-quality images on the Internet and even 4 x 6" prints.

- ✓ **Ringtones:** You can replace the standard ringtone with custom ringtones that you download to your phone. You also can specify different rings for different numbers.

- ✒ **Bluetooth:** The Galaxy S phone supports stereo and standard Bluetooth devices. (See Chapter 3 for more on Bluetooth.)

- ✒ **High-resolution screen:** The Galaxy S phone offers one of the highest-resolution touchscreens on the market (480 x 800 pixels). Figure 1-1 shows off the Super AMOLED display.

- ✒ **Capacitive touch screen:** The Galaxy S phone offers a very slick touch screen that's sensitive enough to allow you to move the screen carefully, but not so sensitive that it's hard to manage.

Figure 1-1: The high-resolution screen with Super AMOLED display.

Taking Your Phone to the Next Level: The Smartphone Features

In addition to the basic capabilities of any entry-level cellphone, the Galaxy S phone has capabilities associated with many popular smartphones, such as the Apple iPhone and the phones based upon Windows Phone 7 OS:

- ✒ **Internet access:** Access Web sites through a Web browser on your phone.

- ✒ **Photos:** The phone comes with a camera, but also the ability to manage photos.

- ✒ **Wireless e-mail:** Send and receive e-mail from your phone.

- ✒ **Multimedia:** Play music and videos on your phone.

✔ **Contact Manager:** The Galaxy S phone lets you take shortcuts from having to enter someone's ten-digit number each time you want to call or text them. In fact, the Contact Manager has the ability to track all the numbers that an individual might have plus their e-mail address and photo. On top of that, it can synchronize with the Contact Manager on both your personal and work PC!

✔ **Digital camcorder:** The Galaxy S phone comes with a built-in digital camcorder that records at a resolution that you can set, including HD.

✔ **Daily Briefing:** The Galaxy S phone tracks your local weather, national news, your schedule, any alarms, and any relevant financial news.

✔ **Mapping and directions:** The Galaxy S phone uses the GPS in your phone to tell you where you are, find local services that you need, and give you directions to where you want to go.

✔ **Business applications:** The Galaxy S can keep you productive while you're away from the office.

I go into each of these capabilities in greater detail in the following sections.

Internet access

Until a few years ago, the only way to access the Internet when you were away from a desk was with a laptop. Smartphones are a great alternative to laptops because they're small, convenient, and ready to launch their Web browsers right away. Even more important, when you have a smartphone, you can access the Internet wherever you are — whether Wi-Fi is available or not.

The drawback to smartphones, though, is that their screen resolution is less than even the most basic laptop screen. Plus, image-heavy Web sites can take a long time to load. To accommodate this problem, more Web sites are adding mobile versions. These sites are slimmed-down versions of their main site with fewer images but similar access to the information on the site. These site names usually begin with m or `mobile`, such as `m.yahoo.com`.

Figure 1-2 shows the regular Web site for Refdesk.com on the left and its mobilized version on the right. The mobilized version has fewer pictures and is more vertically oriented.

On the Galaxy S phone, you can use the mobile version of a Web site if you want, but if you prefer to use the standard Web site, you can pinch and stretch your way to get the information you want — see Chapter 2 for more information on pinching and stretching.

Web   Mobile

Figure 1-2: A mobile Web site is a slimmed-down version of the main site.

For more information on accessing the Internet from your Galaxy S phone, turn to Chapter 7.

Photos

The image application on your phone helps you use the digital camera on your Galaxy S phone to its full potential. Studies have found that cellphone users tend to snap a bunch of pictures within the first month of phone usage. After that, the photos sit on the phone (instead of being downloaded to a computer), and the picture-taking rate drops dramatically.

The Galaxy S phone image management application is different. You can integrate your camera images into your home photo library, as well as photo-sharing sites such as Picasa and Flickr, with minimal effort.

For more on how to use the Photo applications, you can turn to Chapter 10.

Wireless e-mail

On your Galaxy smartphone, you can access your business and personal e-mail accounts, reading and sending e-mail messages on the go. Depending on your e-mail system, you might be able to sync so that when you delete an e-mail on your phone, the e-mail is deleted on your computer at the same time so you don't have to read the same messages on your phone and your computer.

Chapter 6 covers setting up your business and personal e-mail accounts.

Multimedia

Some smartphones allow you to play music and videos on your phone in place of a dedicated MP3 or video player. On the Galaxy S phone, you can use the applications that come with the phone, or you can download applications that offer these capabilities from Android Market.

Chapter 13 covers how to use the multimedia services with your Galaxy S phone.

Business applications

Whether your company gives you a Galaxy S phone for work or you buy your Galaxy S phone yourself, the Galaxy S phone offers you the ability to work on Microsoft Office applications.

Chapter 15 explores how to set up your phone to work with Microsoft Office applications.

Customizing Your Phone with Games and Applications

Application developers — large and small — are working on the Android platform to offer a variety of applications and games for the Galaxy S phone. Unlike most of the other smartphone platforms, Google offers application developers fewer restrictions to what is allowable. This freedom to develop resonates with many developers, resulting in a bonanza of application development on this platform.

As of this writing, more than 100,000 applications are available from the Android Market. For more information about downloading games and applications, turn to Chapters 8 and 9.

Downloading games

Chapter 11 of this book is for gamers. Although your phone comes with a few general-interest games, you can find a whole wide world of games for every skill and taste. In Chapter 11, I give you all the information you need to set up different gaming experiences. Whether you prefer standalone games or multiplayer games, you can set up your Galaxy S phone to get what you need. See Figure 1-3.

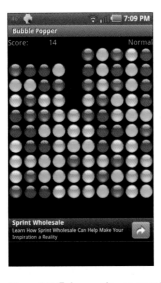

Figure 1-3: Enjoy gaming on your Samsung Galaxy.

Downloading applications

Your phone comes with some very nice applications, but these might not take you as far as you want to go. You might also have some special interests, like philately or star-gazing, that neither Samsung nor your carrier felt would be of sufficient general interest to include it on the phone (can you imagine!).

Take a deep breath

You don't have to rush to implement every feature of your Galaxy S phone the very first day you get it. Instead, pick one capability at a time. Digest it, enjoy it, and then tackle the next one.

I recommend starting with setting up your e-mail and social accounts, but that's just me.

No matter how you tackle the process of setting up your Galaxy S phone, it'll take some time. If you try to cram it all in on the first day, you'll turn what should be fun into drudgery.

The good news is that you own the book that takes you through the process. You can do a chapter or two at a time.

Your phone also comes with preloaded *widgets,* which are smaller applications that serve a particular purpose, such as retrieving particular stock quotes or telling you how your phone's battery is feeling today. They reside on the extended Home screen and are instantly available.

Buying applications allows you to get additional capabilities quickly, easily, and inexpensively. Ultimately, these will make your phone, which is already a reflection of who you are, more personal as you add more capabilities.

What's cool about the Android platform

The Samsung Galaxy S phone is the top-of-the-line Android phone. That means that any application developed for an Android phone will run to its full capability. This is significant because one of the founding principles in the creation of the Android platform is to create an environment where applications developers can be as creative as possible without an oppressive organization dictating what can and cannot be sold (as long as it's within the law, of course). This has inspired many of the best applications developers to go with Android first.

On top of that, Android is designed to run multiple applications at once. Other smartphone platforms have added this capability, but Android is designed for you to be able to jump quickly among multiple apps that you're running — and that makes your experience that much smoother.

You and Your Shadow: Understanding How Your Cellular Carrier Bills You

In the United States, most cellular companies sell phones at a significant discount when you sign up for a service agreement. And most cellular companies offer discounts on phones when you want to upgrade to something newer (as long as you also sign up for another couple of years of service). So, it's not surprising that most people buy their phones directly from cellular companies.

If your new Galaxy S phone device is an upgrade from an older phone, you might have a service plan that was suitable with your last phone but isn't so great anymore. If this is your first cellphone (ever, or with this particular carrier), you might start with an entry-level plan, thinking you won't need "that many minutes," only to find that you and your phone are inseparable, and you need a better plan. The good news is that most cellular carriers allow you to change your service plan.

Most cellular service plans have three components of usage:

- Voice
- Text
- Data

I walk you through each of these components — and how they affect using your Galaxy S — in the following sections.

Voice usage

Voice usage is the most common, costly, and complex element of most service plans. Cellular providers typically offer plans with a certain number of anytime minutes and a certain number of night/weekend minutes. Some providers offer plans with reduced rates (or even free calls) to frequently called numbers, to other cellphones with the same cellular provider, or to other cellphones in general. If you talk a lot, you might be able to opt for an unlimited voice plan (for domestic calls only).

At its core, a Galaxy S phone device is, obviously, a phone. In the early days of smartphones, manufacturers were stung by the criticism that smartphones weren't as easy to use as traditional cellphones. Indeed, you do have to bring up the phone screen to make a call (more on making and receiving calls in Chapter 3). As an improvement, Samsung has made sure that the screen used to make calls is only one click away from the Home screen.

If keeping track of minutes is important to you and your calling plan, be mindful of all those e-mails and social network updates that prompt you to call someone right away. You might be tempted to make more calls than you did with your old (dumb) cellular phone.

Text usage

A texting "bundle" is an add-on to your voice plan. Some service plans include unlimited texting; others offer a certain number of text messages for a flat rate. For example, maybe you pay an additional $5 per month to get 200 free text messages — meaning that combined, you can send and receive *a total* of 200 messages per month. If you go over that limit, you pay a certain amount per message (usually more for text messages you send than those you receive).

As with voice, the Galaxy S phone makes it very convenient to text, making it more likely that you'll use this service and end up using more texts than you expect. However, nothing obligates you to buy a texting plan.

My advice is to get at least some texting capability, but be ready to decide if you want to pay for more or stay with a minimal plan and budget your texts.

Data usage

Although getting texting may be optional, access to the Internet is essential to get the full experience of your Galaxy S phone. The Internet is where you access the capabilities that make the Galaxy S phone so special.

Paying for Internet access on your Galaxy S phone is similar to how you pay an ISP for Internet access for your home computer. Although you can use Wi-Fi to supplement the coverage you get from your cellular carrier, you need to have a data plan from your cellular carrier as well. There's just no getting around it.

Most cellular companies price Internet access with one flat rate. So, when you get Galaxy S, you pay a certain amount per month for data usage (access to the Internet), and it doesn't matter how much you use (or don't use) the Internet on your phone — you still pay that same flat rate.

This is good news: As you customize your phone to keep up with your friends and access your favorite sites, the cost of access won't increase. (Of course, the downside is that if you use the Internet on your phone only a tiny bit, you can't get a cheaper data plan. But then you probably wouldn't be buying a Galaxy S phone device in that case.) Even still, many new smartphone users face sticker shock when they see the cost of their new data plan. Be ready and recognize that it will be worth it!

What if I didn't get my phone from a cellular company?

With a few exceptions, such as an "unlocked" GSM phone, each phone is associated with a particular cellular company. (In this context, a *locked* phone can work only on its original carrier.) Maybe you bought a secondhand phone on eBay, or you got a phone from a friend who didn't want his anymore. If you didn't get your phone directly from a cellular provider, you will need to figure out which provider the phone is associated with and get a service plan from that company. The Galaxy S phones sold in the United States all have the cellular company's logo on the phone printed on the front at the top.

If there is not a logo on the front, you have a "gray market" phone. These are made by Samsung for sale in an international market but have been brought into the United States. These phones are perfectly legal, but you would need to figure out which cellular carrier it can work with. The quickest way is to take the phone to any cellular store; the folks there know how to figure it out.

To narrow down the possibilities on your own, you need to do some investigation. The easiest way is to take off the back of the phone to find the plate with the model and serial number for the phone. If you see IMEI on the plate, the phone is based on a technology called Global System for Mobile (GSM); it'll work with AT&T or T-Mobile (or both). If you see ESN on the plate, the phone will work with either Verizon or Sprint (but not both).

More good news is that your cellular carrier has good data coverage. Although coverage isn't perfect, it's much better than if you were to try to rely on just using free Wi-Fi hotspots.

Don't forget that some Web-based services charge subscription fees. For example, WeatherBug offers a consumer service that gives you weather conditions, but it also offers WeatherBug Pro that provides more information — with a monthly fee to subscribers. Yup, if you want Weatherbug Pro on your phone, you have to pay the piper. Some of these services can be billed through your cellular carrier (check first), but just make sure you're willing to pony up for the service.

Beginning at the Beginning

In This Chapter

▶ Turning on your phone

▶ Charging the phone and managing battery life

▶ Navigating your phone

▶ Turning off your phone and sleep mode

▶ Keeping your phone secure

In this chapter, I fill you in on the basics of using your new Samsung Galaxy. You start by turning on your phone. (I told you I was covering the basics!) I guide you through charging your phone and getting the most out of your phone's battery. Stick with me for a basic tour of your phone's buttons and other features. Then I end by telling you how to turn off your phone or put it in sleep mode.

If you're not new to cellphones in general — and smartphones in particular — you might want to skip this chapter. If the term "smartphone" is foreign to you, you probably haven't used one before, and reading this chapter won't hurt. And, just so you know, a *smartphone* is just a cellular phone on which you can download and run applications that are better than what comes preloaded on a phone right out of the box.

First Things First: Turning On Your Phone

When you open the box of your new phone, the packaging will present you with your phone, wrapped in plastic, readily accessible. If you haven't already, take the phone out of the plastic bag and remove any protective covering material on the screen.

First things first. The On button is on the right side of the phone. You can see the symbol on the button in Figure 2-1. Press the On button for a second, and see whether the screen lights up. Hopefully, your phone arrived with enough electrical charge that you won't have to plug it in to an outlet right away. You can enjoy your new phone for the first day without having to charge it.

On button

Figure 2-1: The On button on the phone.

The phones that you get at the stores of most cellular carriers usually come with the battery installed, partially charged, and registered with the network.

If the screen does light up, don't hold the On button too long, or the phone might turn off.

If the phone screen doesn't light up (rats), you need to charge the battery. Here's the rub: It's important to fully charge the battery for 24 hours, or at least overnight, so that it will last as long as possible. That means that you have to wait to use your beautiful new phone. Sorry.

Of course, it's possible that the battery needs to be inserted in the first place. To do this, you need to open the case. This isn't the end of the world, though. In fact, you should learn to do this sooner or later, anyway, so keep reading to see how.

Note: The Galaxy S has two back styles for different models. Most phones come with a pliable back that you can peel off. The AT&T Captivate (on the AT&T network) has a latching mechanism that holds on the back. The following sections will cover your phone type.

The peel-off back for the Galaxy S

To expose the slots for the optional memory card, SIM card for the T-Mobile Vibrant, and the battery slot, you remove the back by slipping a fingernail under the back cover. There is a small slot to make this easier at the bottom of the phone; see how to do this in Figure 2-2.

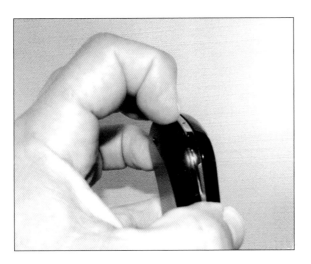

Figure 2-2: Open the cover from the slot at the bottom of your phone.

Don't use a sharp object, like a knife, to peel off the back of the phone. You might get away with that once or twice, but you'll end up scratching the plastic. If you've chewed your nails to the nubbins, ask someone with fingernails to do it for you — or use something plastic, like a credit card.

The latching mechanism on the Captivate

The Captivate uses a latching mechanism. As shown in Figure 2-3, this version of the Galaxy S phone has edges that are angled rather than rounded, as the model has in Figure 2-2. The back part that comes off — the cross-hatched section on which the Galaxy S name is printed — comes off in two steps.

Figure 2-3: The back of the Captivate, closed.

The tricky part is to make the bottom part of the back slide down. Grasp the phone firmly with both hands and push on the bottom part with your thumb, as shown in the left image of Figure 2-4.

If you do this right, the latch will slide down about one-eighth of an inch; see the right image of Figure 2-4. You can then lift off the cross-hatched plastic cover to expose the guts of the phone, as shown in upcoming Figure 2-5.

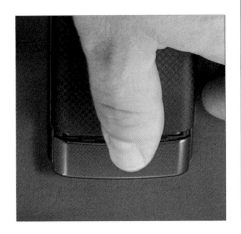

Figure 2-4: Push down the latch on the Captivate.

This cool design hides the seams between the pieces. However, hiding the seams makes it hard the first time you need to get inside! After you know how to get the back off, though, it's very easy.

Now that you have the back off . . .

Without the back, you can see the insides of your phone, as shown in Figure 2-5.

From here, you can insert or remove the following components, as needed:

- The battery.
- The MicroSD card to store files, music, and video (more on this in Chapter 13).
- Your SIM card if you're on a GSM-based cellular network like T-Mobile or AT&T Mobility. (More on SIM cards in Chapter 5.)

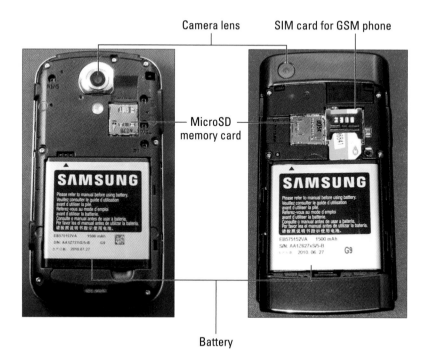

Camera lens   SIM card for GSM phone

MicroSD memory card

Battery

Figure 2-5: The insides of your phone.

The nitty-gritty of how your phone works

As soon as you turn on your phone, several things happen. As the phone is powering up, it begins transmitting information to and receiving information from nearby cellular towers. The first information exchanged includes your phone's electronic serial number. Every cellphone has its own unique serial number built into the hardware of the phone; the serial number in current-generation cellphones can't be duplicated or used by any other phone.

The technical name of this electronic serial number depends on your cellular carrier.

AT&T, T-Mobile, and U.S. Cellular call it an International Mobile Equipment Identity (IMEI) number. Verizon and Sprint refer to it as an electronic serial number (ESN).

It doesn't matter to the phone or the cellular tower if you're near your home when you turn on your phone — and that's the joy of cellphones. All cellular networks have agreements that allow you to use cellular networks in other parts of the country and, sometimes, around the world.

That said, a call outside your cellular provider's own network may be expensive. Within the

United States, many service plans allow you to pay the same rate if you use your phone anywhere in the United States to call anywhere in the United States. If you travel outside the United States, even to Canada, you might end up paying through the nose. Remember: Before you leave on a trip, check with your cellular carrier about your rates. Even if you travel internationally only a few times yearly, a different service plan may work better for you. Your cellular carrier can fill you in on your options. You can read more on billing elsewhere in Chapter 1.

In each case, look for a small engraving or printed image that shows you the correct orientation for the MicroSD card and the SIM card (if you have one). It might be small and faint, but it's there!

Charging Your Phone and Managing Battery Life

Although you probably don't have to plug your phone into an outlet right away, the first time you do plug it in, allow it to charge overnight.

You'll hear all kinds of "battery lore" left over from earlier battery technologies. For example, lithium-ion (Li-ion) batteries don't have a "memory" like nickel-cadmium (NiCad) batteries did. And the Samsung Galaxy S does use Li-ion batteries. That means that you don't have to be careful to allow the battery to fully discharge before recharging it.

Your phone comes with a two-piece battery charger (cable and the transformer), as shown in Figure 2-6.

The cable has two ends: one end that plugs into the phone, and the other that's a standard USB connector. The phone end is a small connector called a micro USB used on some Samsung devices and is becoming the standard for charging cellphones and other small electronics, and for connecting them to computers.

To charge the phone, you have two choices:

- ✔ Plug the transformer into a wall socket and then plug the cable's USB plug into the USB receptacle in the transformer.
- ✔ Plug the USB on the cable into a USB port on your PC.

Then you plug the small end of the cable into the phone. The port is on the top of the phone. It might have a cover over it, but it slides away when you push it with your fingernail. Make sure you push it until it clicks or is all the way to the side, or the charging cable may have a tendency to fall out.

It doesn't really matter in what order you plug in things. However, if you use the USB port on a PC, the PC needs to be powered on for the phone to charge.

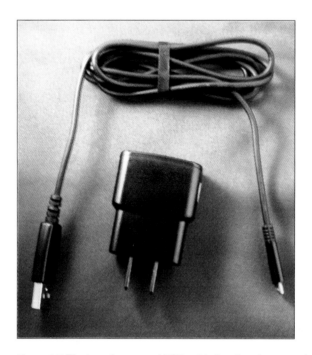

Figure 2-6: The transformer and USB cable for charging your phone.

Unplug the transformer when you aren't charging your phone. A charger left plugged in will draw a small but continuous stream of power.

If your phone is Off when you're charging the battery, an image of a battery will display onscreen for a moment. The green portion of the battery indicates the amount of charge within the battery.

If your phone is On, you see a small battery icon at the top of the screen showing how much charge is in the phone's battery. When the battery in the phone is fully charged, it vibrates to let you know that it's done and that you can unplug the phone.

It takes only a few hours to go from a dead battery to a fully charged battery. Other than the first time you charge the phone, you don't need to wait for the battery to be fully charged. You can partially recharge and run if you want.

In addition to the transformer and USB cable that comes with the phone, you have other optional charging tools:

✔ **Travel USB charger:** If you already have a USB travel charger, you can leave the transformer at home. This will run you about $15. You still need your cable, though any USB-to-micro USB cable should work.

✔ **Car charger:** You can buy a charger with a USB port that plugs into the power socket/cigarette lighter in a car. This is convenient if you spend a lot of time in your car. The list price is $30, but you can get the real Samsung car charger for less at some online stores.

✔ **Photocell or fuel cell charger:** Several companies make products that can charge your phone. Some use photovoltaic cells to transform light into power. Others use a small motor run on fuel. As long as there is a USB port (the female part of the USB) all you need is your cable. These can cost from $40 to $100 on up.

Ideally, use Samsung accessories. And if you don't, make sure that any options you use from the preceding list are from a reputable manufacturer. The power specifications for USB ports are standardized. Reputable manufacturers will comply with these standards, but a less reputable manufacturer might not. Cheap USB chargers will physically fit the USB end of the cable that goes to your phone. However, Li-ion batteries are sensitive to voltage, and an off-brand USB charger can hurt the performance of your battery.

High heat will shorten the life of your battery. Be careful not to leave your phone on your car's dashboard on a summer day. In general, if you keep your phone with you — except when you sit in a sauna or sweat lodge — you'll be safe.

If you take good care of it, your battery should last about two years with a drop in performance of about 25 percent from pristine condition out of the box. At that point, you can replace the battery or upgrade to the newest Galaxy S phone.

Navigating the Galaxy S

Galaxy S phone devices differ from other phones in that they have significantly fewer hardware buttons. In their place is a much heavier reliance on software buttons onscreen.

In this section, I guide you through your phone's buttons, its touchscreen, and the slide-out keyboard (if available on your phone model).

The phone's hardware buttons

Samsung has reduced the number of hardware buttons on the Galaxy S phone device. Most have only two: the Power button and the Volume button. Before you get too far, orient yourself to be sure you're looking at the correct side of the phone. The image in Figure 2-7 shows the phone in vertical orientation and horizontal orientation.

Vertical   Horizontal

Figure 2-7: The Galaxy S in vertical and horizontal orientations.

You'll typically use the phone in its vertical orientation. You can use the Internet in either orientation, though. And you almost always watch videos in the landscape orientation.

Note: When I refer to the left or right of the phone, I'm assuming a vertical orientation.

The Power button

The Power button is on the right side of the phone, when you hold it in vertical orientation, toward the top. Refer to Figure 2-1.

In addition to powering up the phone, pressing the Power button puts the device into sleep mode if you press it for a moment while the phone is on.

Sleep mode shuts off the screen and suspends any running applications. The phone will automatically go into sleep mode after 30 seconds of inactivity to save power, but you might want to do this manually when you put away your phone. The Super AMOLED screen on your Samsung Galaxy S is cool, but it also uses a lot of power.

Don't confuse sleep mode with powering off. Because the screen is the biggest user of power on your phone, having the screen go dark saves battery life. The phone is still alert to any incoming calls; when someone calls, the screen automatically lights up.

The Volume button (s)

Technically, there are two Volume buttons: one to increase the volume, and the other to lower it. Their location is shown in Figure 2-8.

The Volume buttons control the volume of all the audio sources on the phone, including

- The phone ringer for when a call comes in
- The phone headset when you're talking on the phone
- The volume from the digital music and video player

The Volume controls are aware of the context of what volume you're changing. For example, if you're listening to music, adjusting volume raises or lowers the music volume but leaves the ringer and phone earpiece volumes unchanged.

The Volume buttons are complementary to software settings you can make within the applications. For example, you can open the music player software and turn up the volume on the appropriate screen. Then you can use the hardware buttons to turn down the volume, and you'll see the volume setting on the screen go down.

Volume buttons

Figure 2-8: The Galaxy S Volume buttons.

The Camera button on the Sprint Epic 4G

The one exception to the two-hardware-buttons rule is the Sprint Epic 4G. It also has a hardware Camera button, shown in Figure 2-9.

Camera button

Figure 2-9: The Sprint Epic 4G Camera button.

Pressing the Camera button launches the Camera application. On other models, you launch the Camera application from the list of applications.

Pressing this button will also snap the picture, which is a nice little convenience if you're a heavy camera user. In practice, the digital camera is among the most popular features on cellular phones. And, the camera on the Galaxy S is a healthy 5.0 megapixels (MP), providing your shots with sufficient resolution that you can't tell the difference between an analog 35mm camera image and one shot with your Galaxy S.

Read all about the Camera app in Chapter 10.

The touchscreen

To cram all the information that you need onto one screen, Samsung takes the modern approach to screen layout. There are several finger navigation motions that you'll want to become familiar with to work with your screen.

Before diving in, though, here's a small list of terms you need to know:

- **Icon:** This is a little image. Tapping an icon launches an application or performs some function, like making a telephone call.

- **Button:** A button on a touchscreen is meant to look like a three-dimensional button that you would push on, say, a telephone. Buttons are typically labeled to tell you what they will do when you tap them. For example, you'll see buttons labeled Save or Send.

- **Hyperlink:** Sometimes called a link, for short, a hyperlink is text that performs some function when you tap it. Usually, text is lifeless. If you tap a word and it does nothing, it's just text. If you tap a word, and it launches a Web site or causes a screen to pop up, it's a hyperlink.

- **Thumbnail:** This is a small, low-resolution image of a larger, high-resolution picture stored somewhere else.

With this background, it's time to discuss the motions on the touchscreen you'll be using.

You need to clean the touchscreen glass from time to time. The glass on your phone is Gorilla Glass (made by Corning) and is the toughest stuff available to protect against breakage. Use a soft cloth or microfiber to get off fingerprints. You can even wipe the touchscreen on your clothes. However, never use a paper towel! Over time, glass is no match for fibers in the humble paper towel.

Tap

Often, you just tap the screen to make things happen (launch an app) or select options. Think of a tap as like a single click of a mouse on a computer screen. A tap is simply a touch of the screen, much like using a touchscreen at a retail kiosk. Figure 2-10 shows what the tap motion should look like.

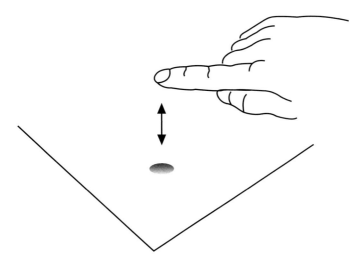

Figure 2-10: The tap motion.

One difference between a mouse click on a computer and a tap on a Galaxy S phone is that a single tap launches applications on the phone in the same way that a double-click of the mouse launches an application on a computer.

A tap is different from "press and hold"; see the next section. If you leave your finger on the screen for more than an instant, the phone thinks that you want to do something other than launch an application.

Press and hold

Press and hold, as the name implies, involves putting your finger on an icon on the screen and leaving it there for more than a second. What happens when you leave your finger on an icon depends upon the situation.

For example, when you press and hold on an application on the Home screen (the screen that comes up after you turn on the phone), a garbage can icon appears at the bottom of the screen. This is to remove that icon from that screen. And when you press and hold an application icon from the list of applications, the phone assumes that you want to copy that application to your Home screen. Don't worry if these distinctions might not make sense yet. The point is that you should be familiar with holding and pressing — and that it's different from tapping.

You don't need to tap or press and hold very hard for the phone to know that you want it to do something. Neither do you need to worry about breaking the glass, even by pressing on it very hard. If you hold the phone in one hand and tap with the other, you'll be fine. I suppose you might break the glass on the phone if you put it on the floor and press up into a one-fingered handstand. I don't recommend this, but if you do try it, please post this on YouTube.

Moving around the screen or to the next screen

Additional finger motions help you move around the screens and to set the screen resolution that you want. Mastering these motions is important to getting the most from your phone.

The first step is navigating the page to access what's not visible onscreen. Think of this as navigating a regular computer screen, where you use a horizontal scroll bar to access information to the right or left of what's visible on your monitor, or a vertical scroll bar to move you up and down on a screen.

The same concept works on your phone. To overcome the practical realities of screen size on a phone that will fit into your pocket, the Galaxy S phone uses a panorama screen layout, meaning that you keep scrolling left or right (or maybe up and down) to access different screens.

In a nutshell, although the full width of a screen is accessible, only the part bounded by the screen of the Galaxy S phone is visible on the display. Depending upon the circumstances, you have several choices on how to get to information not visible on the active screen. These actions include drag, flicks, pinch and stretch, and double taps. I cover all these in the following sections.

Drag

The simplest finger motion on the phone is the drag. You place your finger on a point on the screen and then drag the image with your finger. Then you lift your finger. Figure 2-11 shows what the motion looks like.

Dragging allows you to move slowly around the panorama. This motion is like clicking a scroll bar and moving it slowly.

Flick

To move quickly around the panorama, you can flick the screen to move in the direction of your flick (see Figure 2-12).

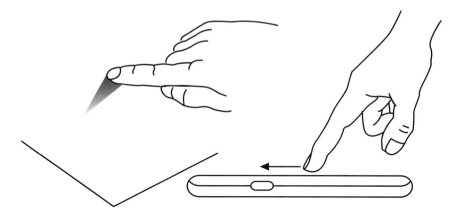

Figure 2-11: The drag motion for controlled movement.

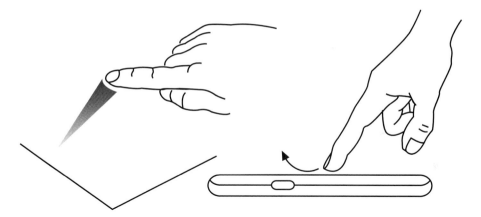

Figure 2-12: Use a flick motion for faster movement.

Better control of this motion will come with practice. In general, the faster the flick, the more the panorama will move. However, some screens, like the extended Home screen, will move only one screen to the right or left no matter how fast you flick.

Pinch and stretch

Some screens allow you to change the resolution of the screen. When this feature is active, the Zoom options change the magnification of the area on the screen. You can zoom out to see more features at a smaller size, or zoom in to see more detail at a larger size.

To zoom out, you put two fingers (apart) on the screen and pull them together to pinch the image. Make sure you're centered on the spot where you want to see in more detail. The pinch motion is shown in Figure 2-13.

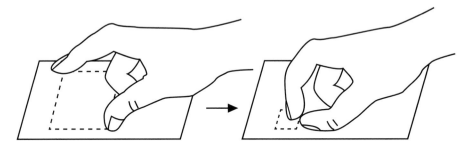

Figure 2-13: Use the pinch motion to zoom out.

The opposite motion is to zoom in. This involves the stretch motion, as shown in Figure 2-14. You place two fingers (close together) and stretch them apart.

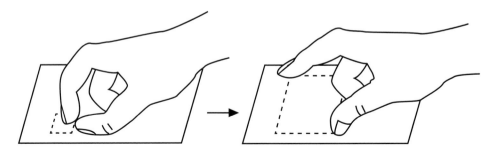

Figure 2-14: Use the stretch motion to zoom in.

Double tap

The double tap (shown in Figure 2-15) just means tapping the same button area on the screen twice in rapid succession. You use the double tap to jump between a zoomed-in and a zoomed-out image to get you back to the previous resolution. This option saves you from any frustration in getting back to a familiar perspective.

Time the taps so that the phone doesn't interpret them as two separate taps. With a little practice, you'll master the timing of the second tap.

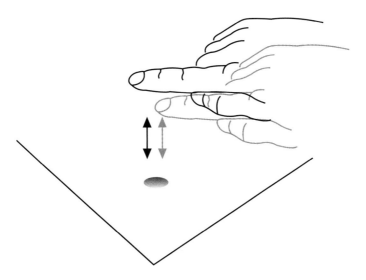

Figure 2-15: The double-tap motion.

The extended Home screen

The extended Home screen (just Home screen, for short) is the first screen that you see when the phone is done setting up. Samsung has set it to be seven screen-widths wide and one screen high.

Figure 2-16 shows a representation of the full Home screen layout. At any given moment, of course, you see only one screen at a time.

Figure 2-16: The Galaxy S phone panorama display of the extended Home screen.

The extended Home screen is where you can organize icons and other functions to best make the phone convenient for you. Out of the box, Samsung and your cellular carrier have worked together to create a starting point for you. Beyond that, though, you have lots of ways that you can customize your Home screen so that you have easy access to the things that are most important for you. Much of the book covers all the things that the phone can do, but a recurring theme is how to put that capability on your Home screen if you wish.

One thing that you cannot customize, though, is the number of screens of the extended Home screen. There are seven. Period. This is the maximum amount of real estate with which you can work. In practice, though, it will take you a while before this feels like much of a limitation.

To start, check out the layout of the Home screen and how it relates to other areas of the phone. Knowing these areas is important for basic navigation.

Figure 2-17 shows a typical Home screen and highlights three important areas on the phone. In most cases, your phone opens to the middle screen, which is the fourth one.

Notification area

Primary shortcuts

Device Function keys

Figure 2-17: Important areas on the Galaxy S phone and Home screen.

✔ **The notification area:** This part of the screen presents you with small icons that let you know if something important is up, like battery life.

✔ **The primary shortcuts:** These four icons remain stationary as you move across the Home screen. Samsung and your cellular carrier have determined that these are the four most important applications on your phone.

✔ **The Device Function keys:** These four keys control essential phone functions, regardless of what else is going on at the moment with the phone. Keep reading for more detail on each area.

There are a series of dots just beneath the notification area on the extended Home screen. The largest dot indicates where you are among the seven screens. In the case of Figure 2-17, the largest dot shows that this is the fourth screen. You can navigate among the screens by dragging the screen to the left or right. This moves you one screen at a time. You can also jump multiple screens by tapping on the dot that corresponds to the screen number you want to see.

Adding shortcuts

The two ways to add a shortcut to your extended Home screen are

✔ Press and hold on an app icon in the Application list

✔ Press and hold a bookmarked Web site

In fact, there are many more things you can add as shortcuts. To consider more, start at the Home screen and follow these steps:

1. **From the extended Home screen, tap the Menu button.**

   This brings up a pop-up at the bottom of the screen, as shown in Figure 2-18.

Figure 2-18: The Menu pop-up from the Home screen.

2. **Tap the Add button.**

   The screen shown in Figure 2-19 appears.

Figure 2-19: The menu of items that you can add to your Home screen.

3. Tap Shortcuts.

I discuss adding widgets in Chapter 8. Among the other items that you can add to your Home screen are

- Contacts that you can quickly call or text
- Telephone numbers from contacts that you can tap and call
- Text addresses that allow you to tap and text
- Directions to a favorite place
- Folders where you've stored Microsoft Office files

4. Tap the Shortcuts selection you want.

You can add shortcuts until the seven pages of your extended Home screen are full by tapping the option you want. It is then placed on that page.

Taking away shortcuts

Taking a shortcut off your Home screen is simple. Press and hold on the screen. In a moment, a garbage can icon appears at the bottom of the screen. Drag the doomed shortcut to the garbage can, and off it goes to its maker.

It is gone, but if you made a mistake, you can get it back easily enough. To re-create it, simply go to the App list, find the icon for the app you just deleted, and press and hold on it. It reappears on your Home screen.

The notification area and screen

As shown in Figure 2-17, the notification area is located at the top of the phone. Here, you see little status icons. Maybe you received a text or an e-mail, or you'll see an application needs some tending to.

Think of the notification area as a special e-mail inbox where your carrier can give you important information about what's happening with your phone. The large icons at the top tell you the condition of the different radio systems on your phone: Green means that they're connected. Gray means that they're not.

You could take the time to learn the meanings of all the little icons that might come up, but that would take you a while. A more convenient option is to press and hold on the notification area for a moment. This allows you to drag down the notification screen, shown in Figure 2-20.

The rest of the screen is written so that you can understand what's going on — and what, if anything, you're expected to do. For example, if you see that you have a new e-mail, you tap the text of the link, and you're taken to your new e-mail.

When you're finished reading the notifications, you slide your finger back up to the top. You can also clear this screen if it gets too full by tapping the Clear button.

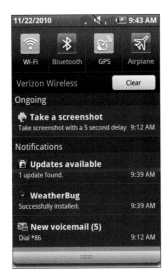

Figure 2-20: Pay attention to the notification screen for important events.

The primary shortcuts

The primary shortcuts are what Samsung and your cellular carrier decided on as the four most important functions of your phone. Each phone type has its own twist on this, but all phones sport a phone icon so that making calls is fast and convenient.

Among the other possible shortcuts here are shortcuts that take you to your contacts, your e-mail, the Internet, texting/messaging, or your list of applications. These shortcuts are not customizable. Don't worry, though. If you want a shortcut to be handy, that's easy to do. I cover how in each chapter.

The Device Function keys

At the bottom of the screen are four important buttons, the Device Function keys. They're always present for you to navigate your phone even though the backlight might switch off to hide their presence. Whatever else you're doing on the phone, these buttons can take over.

From left to right (see Figure 2-21), they are

- Menu
- Home screen
- Back
- Search

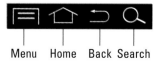

Menu   Home   Back Search

Figure 2-21: The Galaxy S Device Function keys.

The Menu button

Tapping the Menu button brings up a pop-up menu at the bottom of the screen from which you can access valuable capabilities. What's "valuable" depends upon what application is running at that time. For example, Figure 2-22 shows the options you can select from the Home screen.

In Figure 2-22, you can see an icon that lets you add widgets to your Home screen or change the wallpaper. In contrast, tapping the Menu button when you're browsing the Web, as shown in Figure 2-23, brings up options that include bringing up a new browser tab and accessing existing browser tabs.

Figure 2-22: Pop-up options from tapping the Menu button from the Home screen.

Figure 2-23: Pop-up options from tapping the Menu button from a Web browser.

The Home button

Pressing the Home button takes you directly to the extended Home screen. The icon is a silhouette of a house (not a wide arrow, pointing up!).

Tapping this button immediately takes you to the extended Home screen from wherever you are.

The Home button comes in handy when you want to change what you're doing with the phone, such as going from browsing the Web to making a phone call.

The Back button

The Back button on your phone is similar to the Back button in a Web browser: It takes you back one screen.

As you start navigating through the screens on your phone, pressing the Back button takes you back to the previous screen. If you keep pressing the Back button, you'll eventually return to the Home screen.

The Search button

The Search button is a tool you use to find information on your device. The icon looks like a magnifying glass.

When you press the Search button, a Search screen pops up along with a small software keyboard that you use to enter text describing what you want to search for.

The search is based upon the application you're using at the moment. For example, if you're in the Phone application, the Search button searches your telephone book for a contact based on the text that you enter. If you're on the Internet, it searches the Web. If you're on the Home screen, it searches the whole phone.

The keyboard

The screen of the Galaxy S phone is important, but you'll still probably spend more time on the keyboard entering data on a small QWERTY keyboard. All Galaxy S phones come with a software keyboard; the Epic 4G from Sprint comes with a software keyboard *and* a hardware keyboard.

Using the software keyboard

The software keyboard automatically pops up when the application detects a need for user text input. The keyboard appears at the bottom of the screen.

For example, say you're in Seattle, searching for the Seattle Art Museum via the Mapping application. Tap the Search button, and the keyboard pops up onscreen, as shown in Figure 2-24.

Figure 2-24: Use the software keyboard to enter data.

In this case, a text box pops up in addition to the keyboard. As you type **Seattle Art Museum**, the text appears in the box on the screen as if you had typed it on a hardware keyboard. When you tap the Search button, the keyboard disappears, and the location of the Seattle Art Museum is highlighted on your phone. The phone is smart enough to know when the keyboard should appear and disappear. If the keyboard doesn't appear when you want to start typing, you can tap on the text box where you want to enter data.

On the Epic 4G, which has a hardware keyboard, the software keyboard doesn't pop up automatically if the keyboard is extended. If the hardware keyboard is not extended, the software keyboard will pop up when needed.

Using Swype

Galaxy S phones come with an enhanced data-entering capability called Swype. This option automatically comes with your phone, and with a little practice, can dramatically speed your ability to type fast on your phone.

Here's how Swype works: Instead of tapping each discrete key on the keyboard, you leave your finger on the screen and swipe from key to key. The Swype application figures out the words you are wanting to type, including inserting the spaces automatically.

If you like Swype, you can use it any time that you're entering data. If you don't care for it, you can just tap your letters. It's all up to you!

The orientation of the phone

In the earlier section where I discuss the On button, I referred to the phone being in vertical or landscape orientation. The phone senses which direction you're holding the phone, and will orient the screen to make it easier for you to view.

The phone makes its orientation known to the application, but not all applications are designed to change their inherent display. That nuance is left to the writers of the application. For example, your phone can play videos. However, the video player application that comes with your phone shows video in landscape mode only.

In addition, the phone can sense when you are holding it to your ear. When it senses that it is held in this position, it shuts off the screen. You need not be concerned that you will accidentally "chin dial" a number in Botswana.

Going to Sleep Mode/Turning Off the Phone

You can leave your phone on every minute until you're ready to upgrade to the newest Galaxy S phone in a few years, but that will use up your battery in no time. Instead, put your idle phone in sleep mode to save battery power. *Note:* This does happen automatically after 30 seconds of inactivity on the screen.

You can adjust the sleep timer for a longer duration. Or, you can manually put the phone in sleep mode by pressing the Power button for just a moment.

Screen lock (and unlock)

When you want to use your phone again, you need to take two steps. First, you press the On button briefly. This turns on the screen, but you will see that the screen is locked. Each phone has its own particular style to get back to where you were.

- **T-Mobile Vibrant:** Sweep your finger up the screen from bottom to top.

- **Sprint Epic 4G:** Press the image of the lock at the center of the screen and then sweep your finger up or down.

- **AT&T Captivate:** Sweep your finger across the screen in any direction.

- **Verizon Fascinate:** The background of the lock screen is a "mostly completed" puzzle. You unlock the Fascinate by dragging the last puzzle piece into the open space.

Turning off the phone completely

Sometimes it's best to simply shut down the phone if you aren't going to use it for several days or more. To shut down the phone completely, simply press and hold the Power button for a few seconds. The options shown in Figure 2-25 appear:

- ✔ **Silent Mode:** Turn off sound.
- ✔ **Airplane Mode:** Turn off the radio so that you can't receive or make voice calls or send or receive texts or data. As the name implies, use this setting when you're flying, but you want to use applications that can operate without a data connection, such as some games or reading your e-mail.
- ✔ **Power Off:** Shut down the phone completely.

Figure 2-25: The Power-off pop-up screen.

Making Your Phone as Secure as Possible

To make things as simple as possible, Samsung offers a security option that involves remembering a pattern rather than, say, four digits that you enter to unlock the screen. If you set up this security option, you will be presented with a 3 x 3 matrix of dots, as shown in Figure 2-26.

Figure 2-26: The Phone Unlock screen.

To unlock the phone, your finger has to connect any four dots on the screen in a pattern that you program into the phone. Figure 2-27 shows an example unlock pattern.

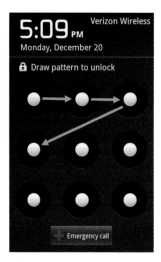

Figure 2-27: Sample phone unlock pattern.

The pattern you choose can be anything as long as it involves at least four different buttons. You can use any given button only once.

Remember your pattern. You have five attempts to get it right before it locks you out. Even if you forget your screen pattern, though, you can still make emergency calls. Contact the customer service department of your cellular carrier in person at a retail store or on another phone to help you get your phone unlocked.

Here's how to set up security on your phone from Settings:

1. **From the Settings home screen, tap Location and Security.**

2. **Tap Set Unlock Pattern.**

   A screen animation explains the pattern options.

3. **View this, following the prompts to enter your pattern twice.**

   If the second entry doesn't match the first, the pattern will turn red. When you enter the pattern the same way twice in a row, the security option will be enabled.

Part II
Communication

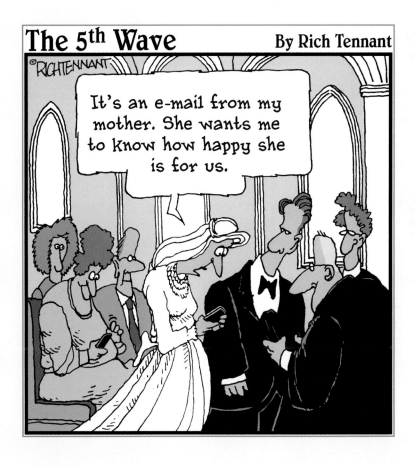

In this part . . .

Your phone is largely about staying connected with the people who are most important to you. A regular cellphone is about talking to and texting with these people. Your Galaxy S phone is about much, much more. You can connect with them through e-mail, social networks, contact databases . . . and, oh yeah, through phone calls and text messages, too. In this part, I show you how.

Calling People

A t its essence, any cellphone — no matter how fancy or smart — exists to make phone calls. The good news is that making and receiving phone calls on your Galaxy S is easy.

In this chapter, I also show you not only how to make a call but how to use your call list to keep track of your calls. And don't skip the section on using your phone for emergencies.

Finally, if you're like many people, you're never doing just one thing at a time, and a Bluetooth headset can make it easier for you to talk on the phone while driving, wrangling kids and dogs, or just plain living life. In this chapter, I show you how to hook up your phone to a Bluetooth headset so you can make and receive phone calls hands-free.

Making Calls

After your phone is on and you're connected to your cellular carrier (see Chapters 1 and 2), you can make a phone call. It all starts from the Home screen (shown in Figure 3-1). Along the bottom of the screen, above the Device Function keys and the Samsung logo, are four icons, which are the *primary shortcuts*. *Note:* You can't move or modify these icons. From left to right, they are (depending on your phone model/carrier):

Osgood Livingston
1-214-555-1212

Voicemail
*86

1-425-555-1212
1-425-555-1212

Winston Churchill
312-555-1212

TIP

✔ **Phone/Dialer**

You won't see Phone *and* Dialer: just one or the other. Likewise for Contacts/Email and Messaging/Browser.

✔ **Contacts/Email**

✔ **Messaging/Browser**

✔ **Applications**

Figure 3-1: Start from the Home screen.

TIP

To help keep things clear, the *phone* is the service, and the *dialer* is the screen with the keypad.

To make a call, follow these steps:

1. **From the Home screen, tap the Phone/Dialer icon.**

   The Dialer screen (see Figure 3-2) appears. This looks like a stylized version of a touch pad on a regular landline phone.

2. **Tap the telephone number you want to call.**

   Don't be alarmed if you don't hear a dial tone until you tap Send; smartphones don't connect to a network and start a dial tone until after you dial your number.

Voicemail   Send   Text message

Figure 3-2: Dial the number from the
Dialer screen.

For long distance calls, you don't need to dial 1 before the area code —
just dial the area code and then the seven-digit phone number.

In Chapter 5, you can read about how to make a phone call through your
contacts.

 3. **Tap the green Send button at the bottom of the screen to place the
    call.**

    Within a few seconds, you should hear the phone ringing at the other
    end or a busy signal.

 4. **When you're done with your call, tap the End button — the red button
    at the bottom of the screen.**

    The call is disconnected.

If the call doesn't go through, either the cellular coverage where you are is
insufficient, or your phone got switched to Airplane mode. It is possible that
your cellular carrier let you out of the door without having set you up for service, but that's pretty unlikely!

Check the notification section of your phone at the top of the screen. If there are no connection strength bars, try moving to another location. If you see a small plane silhouette, bring down the notification screen (see how in Chapter 2) and tap the large plane icon.

Answering Calls

Receiving a call is even easier than making a call. When someone calls you, caller ID information appears along with three buttons. What these three buttons do varies for each phone.

At least one of these buttons allows you to answer. Figure 3-3 shows a typical screen. Tapping the green "whatever" — be it a button, an icon, or a hyperlink — will answer the call.

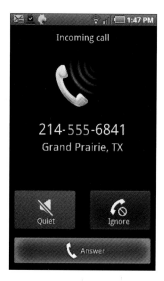

Figure 3-3: The screen when you're receiving a call.

There will also be a red "whatever" (button, icon, or hyperlink). Tapping that will ignore the incoming call and send it to your voicemail.

These two main buttons are pretty standard on any cellular phone. However, your Galaxy S is no standard phone. There is a third option, and what happens depends upon your individual phone.

You can enable (or not) other options when you get a call. For example, you can specify a unique ringtone for a particular number, or have an image of the caller pop up onscreen (if you save your contacts to your phone, rather than a SIM card).

Regardless of what you were doing on the phone at that moment — such as listening to music or playing a game — the answer screen appears. Any active application is suspended until the call is over.

- ✔ **To answer a call:** Tap the Answer button. *Note:* For the Sprint Epic, drag the image of the caller to the option you want to select.

- ✔ **To ignore a call:** Tap the Ignore button, and the caller is sent to your voicemail, where he can leave a message or just hang up.

 You must set up your voicemail for callers to leave you messages. If you haven't yet set up your voicemail, the caller will hear a recorded message saying that your voicemail account isn't yet set up. Some cellular carriers can set up voicemail for you when you activate the account and get the phone; others require you to set up voicemail on your own. Ask how voicemail works at your carrier store or look for instructions in the manual included with your phone.

- ✔ **The third option:** In addition to the standard options of Answer and Ignore buttons when a call comes in, you have one more option — to send the caller a text message. Assuming that your caller is sent to your voicemail, you also can automatically send the caller a text message that acknowledges the call.

 Some of the typical "canned" messages that you can send are

  - I'm driving.
  - In a cinema.
  - I'm in class now.
  - I'm in a meeting.
  - Sorry, I'll call later.

 You tap the message that applies. The message is sent as a text right away, which alerts the caller that you're not ignoring him — it's just that you can't talk right now. Nice touch.

 You can also create and store your own message, like "Go away and leave me alone," or "Whatever I am doing is more important than talking to you." You could also be polite. To create your own canned message, tap the Custom hyperlink and type away. It's then stored on your phone for when you need it.

 This immediate texting works for the Sprint Epic 4G, the T-Mobile Vibrant, and the AT&T Captivate. Sorry Verizon Fascinate users, your third option is to just mute the ringer (the Quiet button; refer to Figure 3-3).

The caller has to be able to receive text messages. This feature doesn't work if your caller is calling from a landline or a cellphone that can't receive texts.

Keeping Track of Your Calls: The Call List

One of the nice features of cellular phones is that the phone keeps a record of the calls that you've made and received. Sure, you might have caller ID on your landline at home or work, but most landline phones don't keep track of who you called. Cellphones, on the other hand, keep track of all the numbers you called. This information can be very convenient, like when you want to return a call, and you don't have that number handy. In addition, you can easily add a number to the contact list on your phone.

By tapping the Call Log icon, you get a list of all incoming and outgoing calls. (This icon, located at the top of the screen, is a phone receiver with arrows pointing to it and away; see Figure 3-4.) Each call bears an icon telling you whether it was an

 ✓ **Outgoing:** An orange arrow points to the number.

 ✓ **Incoming call you received:** A green arrow points away from the number.

 ✓ **Incoming call you missed:** A red phone silhouette with an "x" appears.

A typical call log is shown in Figure 3-4.

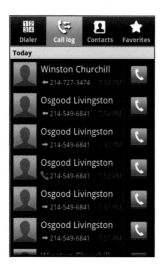

Figure 3-4: A call log.

By tapping any number in your call list (as shown in Figure 3-4), you can do several things:

- ✔ See the date and time the call was logged.

- ✔ Call the number by tapping the green call button.

- ✔ Send a text to that number by tapping the number and then tapping Send Message on the pop-up screen that appears.

- ✔ Mark that number as a favorite by tapping the star icon. Your favorites appears on the Phone/Dialer screen (refer to Figure 3-2), which saves you from having to dial the number.

- ✔ Add the number to your contacts list by pressing and holding on that number. A pop-up gives you the option to add it to your contacts, either by creating a new contact or adding to an existing one. I cover contacts more in Chapter 5.

Making an Emergency Call: The 411 on 911

Cellphones are wonderful tools for calling for help in an emergency. The Samsung Galaxy S, like all phones in the United States and Canada, can make emergency calls to 911 even if your phone isn't registered with a cellular carrier.

Just tap the Phone/Dialer icon on the Home screen, tap 9-1-1, and then tap Send. You'll be routed to the 911 call center nearest to your location. This works wherever you're at within the United States. So, say you live in Chicago but have a car accident in Charlotte; just tap 9-1-1 to be connected to the 911 call center in Charlotte, not Chicago.

Even if your phone isn't registered on a network, you don't have a problem. Your phone will let you know that the only number you can dial is a 911 call center.

When you call 911 from a landline, the address you're calling from is usually displayed for the operator. When you're calling from a cellphone, though, the operator doesn't have that specific information. So, when you call 911, the operator might say, "911. *Where* is your emergency?" Don't let this question throw you; after all, you're probably focused on *what* is happening and not on *where*. Take a moment and come up with a good description of where you are — the street you're on, the nearest cross street (if you know it), any businesses or other landmarks nearby. When the operator knows where you are, she's in a better position to help you with your emergency.

When you accidentally dial 911

If you accidentally dial 911 from your phone, don't hang up. Just tell the operator that it was an accidental call. She might ask some questions to verify that you are, indeed, safe and not being forced to say that your call was an accident.

If you panic and hang up after accidentally dialing 911, you'll get a call from the nearest 911 call center. Answer the call, even if you feel foolish. If you don't answer the call, the 911 call centers will assume that you're in trouble and can't respond. They'll track you down from the GPS in your phone to verify that you're safe. If you thought you'd feel foolish explaining your mistake to a 911 operator, imagine how foolish you'd feel explaining it to the police officer who tracks you down.

When traveling outside the United States or Canada, 911 might not be the number you call in an emergency. Mexico uses 066, 060, or 080, but most tourist areas also accept 911. And most of — but not all of — Europe uses 122. Knowing the local emergency number is as important as knowing the language.

Synching a Bluetooth Headset

With a Bluetooth headset device, you can talk on your phone without needing to hold the phone and without any cords running from the phone to your earpiece. You've probably come across plenty of people talking on Bluetooth headsets. You might even have wondered whether they were a little crazy, talking to themselves. Well, call yourself crazy now, because when you start using a Bluetooth headset, you might never want to go back.

Not surprisingly, Galaxy S phones can connect to Bluetooth devices. The first step to using a Bluetooth headset with your phone is to sync the two devices. Here's how:

1. **From the Home screen on your phone, tap the Application icon.**

   This gets you to the list of all the applications on your phone.

2. **Flick or pan to the Settings icon and tap it.**

   The Settings icon is shown in Figure 3-5. This screen holds most of the settings that you can adjust on your phone.

3. **Tap the Wireless and Network icon.**

   This opens a number of setting options that relate to the cellular network, Wi-Fi networking options, and roaming capabilities.

Settings

Figure 3-5: The Settings icon in the Applications list.

4. **Tap Bluetooth Settings.**

The Bluetooth Settings screen appears, as shown in Figure 3-6.

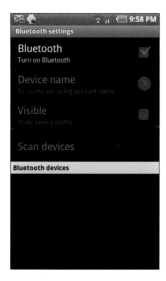

Figure 3-6: The Bluetooth Settings screen.

5. **Enable the Bluetooth radio if it's not already.**

Your phone probably came out of the box with the Bluetooth radio set to Off. Keeping it off when you don't use it does save battery life. You can tell whether the Bluetooth radio is on if the Bluetooth icon appears in the notification area at the top of the screen.

If you don't see a check mark next to the word Bluetooth, tap the check box.

6. **Tap the word Visible.**

This enables your phone to be seen by other Bluetooth devices. This state will last for 120 seconds. That is enough time for you to get your Bluetooth device into pairing mode and negotiate the proper security settings.

7. **Tap the words Scan Devices.**

Your phone scans the area for other Bluetooth devices.

8. **Put your headset into synching mode.**

Follow the instructions that came with your headset.

After a moment, the phone will "see" the headset. When it does, you're prompted to enter the security code, and the software keyboard will pop up.

9. **Enter the security code for your headset and then tap the Enter button.**

The security code on most headsets is 0000, but check the instructions that came with your headset if that number doesn't work.

Your phone might see other devices in the immediate area. If so, it will ask you which device you want to pair with. Tap the name of your headset.

Your headset is now synched to your phone. If your headset is on when the other Bluetooth device is already on, they'll recognize each other and automatically pair up from now on.

The Joy of Text

In This Chapter

▶ Sending a text message

▶ Sending a text message with an attachment

▶ Receiving a text message

Sure, cellphones are made for talking. But these days, many people use their cellphones even more for texting. *Text messages* (short messages, usually 160 characters or less, sent by cellphone) are particularly convenient when you can't talk at the moment (maybe you're in a meeting or class) or when you just have a small bit of information to share ("Running late — see you soon!").

Many cellphone users — particularly younger ones — prefer sending texts to making a phone call. They find texting a faster and more convenient way to communicate, and they often use texting shorthand to fit more "content" in that character limit.

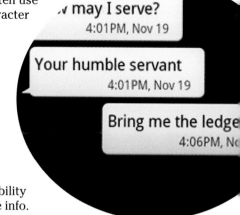

Even the most basic phones support texting these days, but your Galaxy S phone makes sending and receiving text messages more convenient, no matter whether you're an occasional or pathological texter. In this chapter, I fill you in on how to send a text message (with or without an attachment), how to receive a text message, and how to read your old text messages.

To use text messaging, you must have texting capability as part of your service plan. See Chapter 1 for more info.

Sending a Text Message

When you're ready to brag about your new Galaxy S phone and want to send a text to your best friend, here's how easy it is:

1. **On the Home screen, tap the Messaging icon (shown in Figure 4-1).**

   Most of the Galaxy S phones have messaging as one of the primary shortcuts. The exception is AT&T. AT&T selected messaging to be on the center Home screen, so it's right there when you turn on your phone.

   The two styles used for the messaging application are shown in Figure 4-1.

   Figure 4-1: Open messaging with one of these icons.

2. **Tap the New Message link.**

   You move to the texting screen shown in Figure 4-2. A text box appears at the top of the screen with the familiar To field at the top. The software keyboard will pop up when you tap in the Type to Compose text box (unless you've extended your slide-out keyboard on the Sprint Epic 4G).

3. **Tap to enter the ten-digit mobile telephone number of the recipient.**

   Be sure to include the area code, even if the person you are texting is local. However, there is no need to put a "1" before the number.

   If this is your first text, you haven't had a chance to build up a history of texts. After you've been using your messaging application for a while, you will have entered contact information. Click the Recent, Contacts, and Group buttons to save you from entering a complete ten-digit number. I cover how this works in later chapters.

4. **Tap the message in the Type to Compose text box.**

   Your text message can be up to 160 characters, including spaces and punctuation.

5. **Send the text by tapping the Send button to the right of your message.**

   The phone takes it from here. Within a few seconds, the message is sent to your friend's cellphone.

Figure 4-2: Write your text here.

After you build your contact list (read about this in Chapter 5), you can tap a name. If there's only one number for that contact, your phone assumes that's the receiving phone you want to send a text to. If that contact has multiple numbers, it asks you which phone number you want to send your text to.

You've probably heard a thousand times about how it is a very bad idea to text while you are driving. Here comes one-thousand-and-one. It is a *very bad idea* to text while you are driving — and illegal in some places.

Carrying on a Conversation via Texting

In the bad ol' pre-Galaxy S days, most cellular phones would keep a log of your texts. The phone would keep each text that you sent or received in sequential order.

Texts stored sequentially are old school. Your Galaxy S keeps track of the contact with which you have been texting and puts it into a "conversation."

In Figure 4-3, you can see that the first page for messaging refers to *conversations.* After you start texting someone, those texts are stored in one conversation. When you start a texting conversation with someone else, there is a second conversation.

As Figure 4-3 shows, each text message is presented in sequence, with the author of the text indicated by the direction of the text balloon.

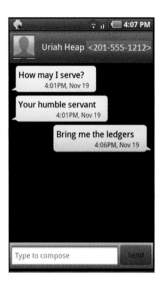

Figure 4-3: A messaging conversation.

Note the Type to Compose text box at the bottom of the screen. With this convenient feature, you can send whatever you type to the person with whom you're having a conversation.

Sending an Attachment with a Text

What if you want to send something in addition to or instead of text? Say, you want to send a picture, some music, or a Word document along with your text. Easy as pie, as long as the phone on the receiving end can recognize the attachment.

1. **Open a new message, identify your recipient, and compose your text, as explained earlier in this chapter.**

2. **Tap the Menu button and tap Attach (see Figure 4-4) to attach a file.**

    You'll be asked what kind of file you want to attach; see Figure 4-5. Your choices include pictures, videos, and audio files.

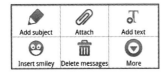

Figure 4-4: Tap the Attach button to attach a file to a text.

Figure 4-5: Choose what type of file you want to attach.

3. **Tap your file type choice, and your phone presents you with the options that fall into that category.**

4. **Tap Select.**

   The attachment becomes a part of your text message.

5. **Continue typing your text message, if needed.**

6. **When you're done with the text portion of the message, tap the Send button, and off it goes.**

A simple text message is an SMS (short message service) message. When you add an attachment, you're sending an MMS (multimedia messaging service) message. Back in the day, MMS messages cost more to send and receive than SMS messages did. These days, that isn't the case in the United States.

Receiving Text Messages

Receiving a text is even easier than sending one.

When you're having a text conversation and you receive a new text from the person you're texting with, your phone signals that you have a message. It will beep, or it will vibrate if you have the sound off. Also, the notification area of the screen (the very top) will indicate that you have a text by showing a very small version of the messaging icon (refer to Figure 4-1). Pull down the notification screen to get more information, as shown in Figure 4-6.

Notification screen

Figure 4-6: Notification screen when text messages are received.

If an attachment comes along, it's included in the conversation. You can see an example in Figure 4-7.

To access the text, you need to unlock the screen. The messaging icon, an envelope, will also have the number of new texts that you have. Tap that icon to open the conversations.

Figure 4-7: A texting conversation with an attachment.

Managing Your Text History

The Messaging Conversations screen stores and organizes all your texts until you delete them. You will want to clean up this screen every now and then.

The simplest option for managing your messages is to tap the Menu icon and then tap Delete Threads. You can then select and unselect all the conversations that you want deleted. Tap the Delete link at the bottom of the screen, and they disappear.

Practice good texting hygiene. Regularly clear out older texts. It's highly unlikely that you need to keep 200 texts from anyone. Starting a new conversation is easy enough, anyway.

Another deletion option is to open the conversation. You can delete each text by pressing and holding on the balloon. After a moment, a menu appears from which you can delete that message. This method is a lot slower if you have lots of texts, though.

I recommend you be vicious in deleting the older texts and conversations. Trust me; deleting all your messages can be cathartic!

Managing Your Contacts

In This Chapter

▶ Putting all your callers and texters on your phone

▶ Getting all your contacts in one location

▶ Keeping up to date with just a few taps

Y ou're probably familiar with using contact databases. Many cellphones automatically create one, or at least prompt you to create one. You also probably have a file of contacts on your work computer, comprising work e-mail addresses and telephone numbers. And if you have a personal e-mail account, you probably have a contact database of e-mail accounts of friends and family members. If you're kickin' it old school, you might even keep a paper address book with names, addresses, and telephone numbers.

The problem with having all these contact databases is that it's rarely ever as neat and tidy as I've just outlined. A friend might e-mail you at work, so you have her in both your contact databases. Then her e-mail address might change, and you update that information in your personal address book but not in your work one. Before long, you have duplicated contacts and out-of-date contacts, and it's hard to tell which is correct. How you include Facebook or LinkedIn messaging in your contact profile is unclear.

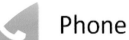

In addition to problems keeping all your contact databases current, it can be a hassle to migrate the database from your old phone. Some cellular carriers or firms have offered a service that converts your existing files to your new phone, but it's rarely a truly satisfying experience. You end up spending a lot of time correcting the assumptions it makes.

You now face that dilemma again with your Galaxy S of deciding how to manage your contacts. The purpose of this chapter is to give you the information on the advantages of each approach so that you can decide which one will work best for you. That way, you won't have the frustration of wishing you had done it another way before you put 500 of your best friends in the wrong filing system.

Deciding Where to Store Contacts

Depending upon your phone, you have two or three choices for creating contacts. These include saving contact information on

- Your phone
- Your Gmail account
- SIM card

If you have an AT&T Captivate or a T-Mobile Vibrant, you can also store your contacts on your SIM card.

The good news is that you can use tools on your phone to copy your contacts from one format to another. The reality, though, is that you'll probably do this about as often as you change the batteries in your smoke detector and back up your computer files. In other words, you probably won't do this as often as you should.

So, pick one option as your primary option for storing your contacts and keep that current. Then, when you do get around to checking your tire pressure and cleaning out the gutters, it would be a good time to also synchronize your contact databases.

The next sections present the advantages for each method so that you can decide which approach will be your primary storage method. I start with the SIM card because this is the most basic option. I then look at the advantages of storing contact information on the phone and then on your Gmail account. Later in the chapter, in the section "Creating Contacts within Your Database," I show you how to add contacts manually.

Using the SIM card: Captivate and Vibrant users

A *SIM card* is a special memory card used with phones that operate using Global System for Mobile Communications (GSM) technology, which is a digital cellular standard from Europe. AT&T Mobility and T-Mobile use this platform for their cellular networks. You can see how small a SIM card is in Figure 5-1.

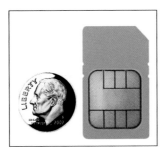

Figure 5-1: A SIM card.

A SIM card stores the information on your cellular number as well as basic information on your contacts. This allows you to switch phones with ease by simply removing the SIM card from one phone and moving it to the next.

Given all the cool things about your new Samsung Galaxy S, it's hard to imagine that you will ever want to or need to upgrade your phone. Someday this will happen, however. (Then again, you might be a serial phone user, and switch phones to match your outfit.)

The content of a contact on a SIM card includes

- Contact name, including first and last name
- Telephone number
- E-mail address

Using the Galaxy S contact database

Your Samsung Galaxy S has a very powerful and convenient contact database for use on your phone. Its icon is either one of your primary shortcuts with the icon just above the Device Function keys or one of the icons on the center Home screen. The image of the icon is shown in Figure 5-2.

Defining this database as being on your "phone" is a little misleading. Technically, your SIM card is in your phone, too. Just go with it for now.

This database, and the Contacts application that manages the data, does more than just store names, phone numbers, and e-mail addresses. It also includes the following format.

Figure 5-2: The
Contacts icon.

- ✓ The first and last name of the contact in separate fields
- ✓ All telephone numbers, including
  - Mobile
  - Home
  - Work
  - Work Fax
  - Pager
  - The number for their assistant or back-up
  - Other
- ✓ E-mail addresses
  - Home
  - Work
  - Mobile
- ✓ Up to nine IM addresses, including all the largest IM services (such as Google Talk, AIM, Windows Live, and Yahoo!)
- ✓ Company
- ✓ Job Title
- ✓ Nickname
- ✓ Mailing address for
  - Home
  - Work
  - Another location
- ✓ Any notes about this person
  - Web address
  - Birthday
  - Anniversary

Fortunately, the only essential information is a name. Every other field is optional.

Then, as if this wasn't enough, you can assign a custom ringtone to play when this person contacts you. I cover the steps to assign a music file to an individual caller in Chapter 13.

Finally, you can assign a picture for the contact. It can be one out of your Gallery; you can take a new picture; or as I discuss later in this chapter, you can connect a social network, like Facebook, which will then use that contact profile picture.

To add a picture of a person to your contacts list from your Gallery, you open that profile, tap Menu, and edit the contact. A screen like the one shown in Figure 5-3 will show a generic silhouette with a plus sign. Tapping the plus sign opens the Gallery app and allows you to choose a picture in place of the generic silhouette.

Figure 5-3: A contact being edited.

Using a Gmail contact database

Another option to consider is using the Contact Manager that comes with your Gmail account. If you've been a Gmail user for a while, chances are that you already have a contact database that's mostly populated with e-mail addresses.

The contact database in your Gmail account has almost exactly the same fields as on your phone. It doesn't include the custom ringtone and a few other details. However, they link together nicely.

Here are some good reasons why you'd want to use a database not stored on your phone as your primary database:

- You don't lose your database if you lose your phone.

- If more of your social time is spent on your computer and you use your phone only occasionally, having the database on your computer be the most accurate is probably more valuable.

- As nice as the keyboard and screen are on the Galaxy S, it's easier to make additions, changes, and deletions to a database when you use a full keyboard and large screen.

Synchronizing Your Contact Databases

After you decide how you want to import contact information to your Galaxy S phone, actually doing it is a breeze. Better still, you're not just importing a contact database, but synching it with its host, like your PC or Gmail account. The next sections cover the combinations of synching options.

Even in the best situations, automatic synching of databases is imperfect. Don't be surprised to find errors.

Synching between your SIM and your phone contacts

This method applies to AT&T Captivate and T-Mobile Vibrant phone users because those are the only Galaxy S models that use SIM cards.

1. **Tap the Contacts icon on the Home screen.**

   This brings up your current contacts. A contact database is shown in Figure 5-4.

2. **Tap the Menu icon of the Device Function keys.**

3. **Tap the More option.**

   This brings up a pop-up screen with many options.

4. **Tap the SIM Management hyperlink.**

5. **Carefully select the option that copies in the direction you want the information to flow; choices are shown in Figure 5-5.**

   For a new phone, you want to copy your existing SIM contact database to the Contact Manager on your phone. When you want to copy the information in the Contacts application to your SIM so you can use it on another phone, copy your contacts to SIM.

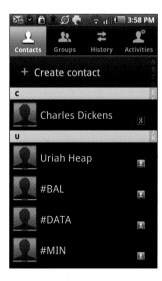

Figure 5-4: A contact database.

Figure 5-5: The SIM management options.

6. **Select the contacts you wish to copy over by tapping the check box shown in Figure 5-6 next to the appropriate name.**

   You can also just opt for Select All to copy all the contacts.

   The phone might warn you that some data will be lost. This is because the SIM records are smaller than what the phone stores.

7. **Accept the data loss.**

   The records are automatically copied.

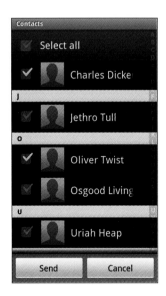

Figure 5-6: Saving selected contacts options.

Synching between your phone contacts and Gmail

Here is where things get so easy it's a little scary. All you need to do is tell the phone that it's okay to synchronize with Gmail; then enter your password. Really — that's it! From that point, it synchronizes everything automatically.

You're not required to set up automatic synching if you don't want it. My bet, though, is that you do. Yeah, this does use some battery life, but the convenience is worth it.

1. **Tap the Contacts icon on the Home screen.**

   This brings up your current contacts; refer to Figure 5-4.

2. **Tap the Menu icon of the Device Function keys.**

3. **Tap the Accounts icon.**

   If the option for Accounts doesn't appear on this pop-up, tap More, and the Accounts hyperlink will appear. This screen is shown in Figure 5-7.

Figure 5-7: The Accounts and Sync menu.

4. **Make sure that the Background Data and the Auto-sync check boxes are marked. Then tap the Add Account button (at the bottom of the screen).**

The Add an Account screen opens, as shown in Figure 5-8.

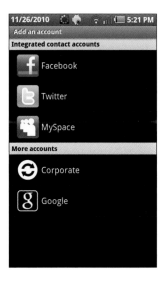

Figure 5-8: Add an account here.

You see lots of options of accounts that you can add. I'll dive into these later.

5. Select Google.

This brings up the information screen shown in Figure 5-9.

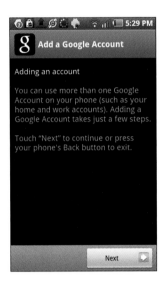

Figure 5-9: The Add a Google Account screen.

6. Tap Next.

This brings up the create/sign in screen shown in Figure 5-10.

7. Select the option as to whether you have a Gmail account.

To use Android Market, you need to have a Gmail account, anyway. You need one here if you are going to sync with it (obviously). If you don't have a Gmail account, now is a great time to get one. For these steps, I assume that you have one.

8. Tap Sign In (see Figure 5-10).

This brings up the sign-in screen shown in Figure 5-11.

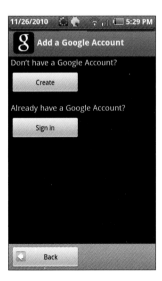

Figure 5-10: Create a Google account here.

Figure 5-11: The Google account sign-in screen.

9. **Enter your account ID and password.**

You'll be asked to accept the terms and conditions. Go ahead. The phone and the Google server will do some communications back and forth, and then return with a screen like that shown in Figure 5-12.

Within a few seconds of finishing, your phone and Gmail will be chatting away, sharing all your contacts. And while they're at it, they're also sharing all your e-mails and events (appointments). More on these topics in Chapters 6 and 14.

Then, when the phone and Gmail are done talking, all the contacts from your phone are on your Gmail account, and all the contacts from your Gmail account are on your phone. Sweet.

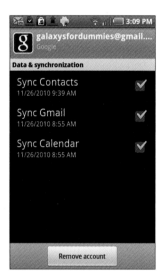

Figure 5-12: The Data & Synchronization screen.

What's even cooler is that when you update a contact on your phone, it automatically lets your Gmail account know. And when you update your Gmail account, it lets your phone know. You set this up when you tap Background Data and Auto-sync in Step 4 of the preceding list.

You can tell where a contact is stored by looking at the contact within your phone's database. Looking at Figure 5-4, you can see a small "g" on the contact for Charles Dickens. That means that the contact is from my Gmail account. The small orange icon for Contacts next to Uriah Heap shows that he is stored on my phone.

Creating Contacts within Your Database

You might wonder why I waited this long into the chapter before telling you how to create a contact. Well, I assume that you'd rather populate as much of your phone's contact database as possible by using the automated tools.

Going forward, of course, you'll get messages from people who haven't contacted you before. You will also meet people whom you want to add to your contacts. This section goes through the steps to add them to your contacts.

Adding contacts as you communicate

When you receive a call, a text, or an e-mail from someone who isn't in your contact list, you're given the option to create a profile for that person. The same is true when you initiate contact with someone who isn't in your contact list. Figure 5-13 shows the phone with a number dialed. After you enter the complete number, you have the option to Add to Contacts.

When you tap Add to Contacts, you're immediately given the option to create a contact or update an existing contact. Your phone doesn't know whether this is a new number for an existing contact or a totally new person. Rather than make an assumption (like how lesser phones on the market would do), your phone asks you whether you need to create a new profile or add this to an existing profile.

When you select New Contact, your phone then asks you where you want to save the profile. If you have a SIM card, the pop-up looks like the image in Figure 5-14. If you don't have a SIM card, you see the options that do apply, such as phone or your primary e-mail account.

Figure 5-13: The Add to Contacts option.

Figure 5-14: The Save Contact To pop-up.

When you select your storage location, the profile template is populated with that number. Then, add the name and any other contact information associated with that number.

Similarly, when you're working with texts or e-mails (more in Chapter 6), if your phone doesn't recognize an address, an icon appears allowing you to create a profile for that person.

Adding contacts manually

Adding contacts manually involves taking an existing contact database and entering its entries to your phone, one profile at a time. (This option, a last resort, was the only option for phones back in the day.)

1. **Tap the Contacts icon.**

   This brings up the screen shown in Figure 5-4.

2. **Tap Create Contact.**

   A screen with text boxes appears. This is the profile for the contact.

3. **Fill in the information that you want to include.**

4. **Tap Save.**

   The profile is now on your phone. Repeat the process for as many profiles as you want to create.

Adding Facebook contacts

To add Facebook to your Contacts, go into your Contacts application by tapping your Home screen or App list. From here

1. **Tap the Add Account button.**

   The screen shown in Figure 5-15 appears. This is a list of the services that are set up to integrate easily with contacts.

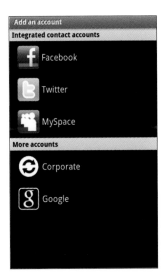

Figure 5-15: The services that can populate your Contacts.

2. **Tap the Facebook icon.**

   You'll be asked for your Facebook ID and password. Enter it. Depending upon your phone, Facebook might check you for permission.

3. **Choose how often to sync your phone with Facebook.**

   I suggest once every 24 hours, but you can sync as often as every hour.

4. **Choose whether you want all your contacts or just selected ones.**

   You can put your entire list of Facebook friends into your Contacts app, but this could make your contact list difficult to manage. You can select who goes into your contact database by selecting the check box next to each contact name.

5. **Tap Done.**

   Your Contacts list will be populated with friends from Facebook.

How Contacts Make Life Easy

Phew. Heavy lifting over. After you populate the profiles of dozens or hundreds of contacts, you're rewarded with a great deal of convenience.

Start by tapping a contact. You see that person's profile, as shown in Figure 5-16.

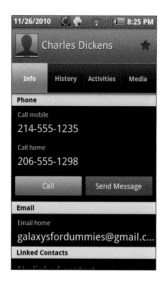

Figure 5-16: A basic contact profile.

All the options you have for contacting this contact are but one simple tap away:

- ✔ Tap a telephone number to dial that number.

- ✔ Tap the e-mail address to create an e-mail (well, after you're set up for e-mail, as discussed in Chapter 6).

- ✔ Tap the green Call button, and the phone asks you which number you want to dial (assuming that there is a choice). You choose, and the phone dials the number.

- ✔ Tap the gray Send Message button, and the phone asks you which number you want to text (again, if there is a choice). You choose, and the phone brings up the text screen.

- ✔ To Instant Message that person, tap her IM address. The phone will bring up the IM application.

About the only thing that tapping on a data field won't do is print an envelope for you if you tap the mailing address!

Playing favorites

Over the course of time, you probably find yourself calling some people more than others. It would be nice to not have to scroll through your entire contacts database to find those certain people. Contacts allows you to place some of your contacts into a Favorites list for easy access.

From within the Contacts app, open the profile by tapping that person's name (refer to Figure 5-16).

To the right of the contact name is a star. If that star is gold, that Contact is a Favorite. If not, not. Tap the star to make that contact a Favorite.

You won't immediately see a difference in your Contacts other than the appearance of the gold star. When you open your Phone/Dialer, however, this contact now appears under your Favorites tab. This is shown in Figure 5-17.

You can immediately find your Favorites from this tab and then dial that person by tapping his name and tapping Send.

Sending e-mails from your contacts

One of the focus areas that Samsung spent a lot of time considering when creating this version of Samsung Galaxy S phone is to make it easier for you to communicate with your most important contacts: family, friends, co-workers, customers, or whoever matters to you.

The gold star designates this
contact as a Favorite.

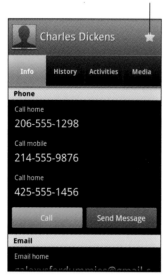

Figure 5-17: Contacts on the Favorites
tab in Phone/Dialer.

On most smartphones, including the Samsung Galaxy S phone, you can communicate with someone by going to their contact profile. From the contact profile, you can quickly send an e-mail by just tapping that contact's email address. Up pops the composition screen with the e-mail address prefilled in the To field. In this case, the e-mail will come from your default e-mail account.

Sending and Receiving E-Mail

In This Chapter

▶ Setting up e-mail accounts on your phone

▶ Reading e-mail on your phone

▶ Sending e-mail from your phone

*I*f you've had e-mail on your phone for a while, you know how convenient it is. If your Galaxy S phone is your first cellphone with the capability to send and receive e-mail, prepare to be hooked.

I start this chapter by showing you how to set up your e-mail, regardless of whether your e-mail is supported (more on that in a bit). Then I show you how to read your e-mails. Finally, I tell you how to write and send e-mails.

Your phone primarily interacts with your inbox on your e-mail account. It isn't really set up to work like the full-featured e-mail application on your computer, though. Theoretically, you might never need to get on your computer to access your e-mail again, and you could store e-mails in folders on your phone. However, the phone access to e-mail is best used in working with the e-mails that are in your inbox.

Using e-mail on your phone requires a data connection. Some cellular carriers solve this problem by obliging you to have a data plan with your phone. If your cellular carrier does not, you won't be able to use e-mail unless you're connected to a Wi-Fi hotspot.

Setting Up Your E-Mail

Your phone can manage up to ten e-mail accounts from the Email app on your phone. With a Galaxy phone (unlike some other phones), you don't need to create a separate e-mail account just for your phone. However, you might want to set up a new Gmail account if you don't have one already (more on that later).

The Email app on your phone routinely polls all the e-mail systems for which you give an e-mail account and password. It then presents you with a copy of your e-mails.

Setup is so easy and makes you so productive, that I advise you to consider adding all your e-mail accounts.

In general, connecting to a personal e-mail account simply involves telling your phone the name of your e-mail account and its password. (For your office e-mail account, you probably will need to consult with your IT department for some extra information.) As long as your account is reasonably modern, the phone and your e-mail system can talk to each other and share away. Just to be sure, though, keep reading to see how.

Using your Gmail account

If you've read Chapter 5 on how to set up contacts, and your main e-mail account is on Gmail, you may already be a winner! In that chapter, I show you how to synchronize contacts between your phone and your Gmail e-mail.

If you want access to only your Gmail account, you're done. Skip the next section. As long as you follow the recommended setup — specifically, having your phone (in the background) routinely poll the Gmail server for new messages — you're all set.

The advantages of getting a Gmail account

You might already have a work and a personal e-mail account. You might even have an old e-mail account that you check only once in a while because some friends, for whatever reason, haven't updated their profile for you and continue to use an old address.

The thought of getting yet another e-mail address, even one that's free, might (understandably) be unappealing. After all, it's just another address and password to remember. However, some important functions on your phone require that you have a Gmail account.

These include

- Buying applications from Android Market. (This is huge!) I go over Android Market in Chapter 9.

- Free access to the photo site Picasa (although other sites have many of the same features). I cover Picasa and photo options in Chapter 10.

- Access to the Media Hub. This is a slick service explained in Chapter 13.

Long story short, it's worth the trouble to get a Gmail account, even if you already have a personal e-mail account.

Working with non-Gmail e-mail accounts

Your phone is set up to work with up to ten e-mail accounts. If you have more than ten accounts, I'm thinking that you might have too much going on in your life. No phone, not even the Galaxy S, can help you there!

To set up an e-mail account other than Gmail to work with your phone, go to the Home screen. Look for the Mail icon; it has an envelope icon on it (see Figure 6-1). You may also find Mail as one of your four primary shortcuts that are just above the Device Function keys.

Figure 6-1:
The Mail icon.

After setup, the first Email screen will have all your e-mails from all your e-mail accounts. Until you do, the screen will have nothing but placeholders.

Make sure that your phone is actively connected to the Internet by checking your notification screen (the line along the top with the icons). If you get no indication that the phone is trying to sync, go to the notifications screen to verify that your cellular and/or wireless connections are operating.

You need to have an active wireless connection when you're setting up your e-mail accounts. If your phone and the e-mail server can't make a connection, the phone can't verify that these accounts are spelled properly and that you entered the correct passwords.

1. **Tap the Menu icon from the Email screen.**

   This brings up a pop-up menu that looks something like the image shown in Figure 6-2.

2. **Tap the Accounts icon.**

3. **Tap the Menu icon on the Email account screen.**

   Tapping this icon brings up two options in the pop-up: Compose and Add Account.

4. **Tap the Add Account icon.**

   This brings up the screen shown in Figure 6-3.

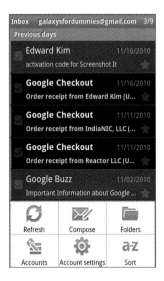

Figure 6-2: The menu pop-up for the Email app.

Figure 6-3: The Set up Email account screen.

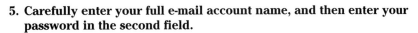

5. **Carefully enter your full e-mail account name, and then enter your password in the second field.**

Your e-mail address should include the full shebang, including the @ sign and everything that follows it. Make sure to enter your password correctly, being careful with capitalization if your e-mail server is case sensitive — most are. If in doubt, select the option to let you see your password.

6. **Decide whether you want this account to be your default e-mail account.**

After you add multiple accounts to your phone, only one account can be your primary, or default, account. Although you can send an e-mail from any of the accounts registered on your phone, you have to select one as the default. If you want this account to be the primary or default account, select the Send Email from This Account by Default check box. If not, leave that option as it is.

7. **Tap Next. (The Next button is on the screen, but behind the keyboard.)**

You get a Warning pop-up screen like that shown in Figure 6-4. Do not worry about this warning. It is for advanced situations.

8. **Tap OK.**

Figure 6-4: Tap through the warning.

If everything goes as planned, your phone and your e-mail account will start chatting. Within a few seconds, you get a screen like that shown in Figure 6-5.

Figure 6-5: Name your e-mail
account and add a signature.

9. **Enter names for the new e-mail account.**

You can always use the e-mail address for the name, but I recommend
choosing something shorter, like Joe's MSN or My Hotmail. The second
name will automatically be entered as your signature at the end of your
e-mails from this account.

10. **Tap Done.**

Don't forget to check that everything has gone as planned and is set up to
your liking. Just go back to the Home screen and tap Email.

Using Figure 6-6 as an example, you can see that I have two accounts registered on my phone. It worked!

Setting up a business e-mail account

In addition to personal e-mail accounts, you can add your work e-mail to your
phone — if it's based upon a Microsoft Exchange server, that is, and okay
with your company's IT department.

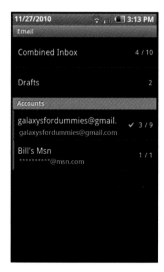

Figure 6-6: The Email Home screen with two accounts.

Before you get started, you need some information from the IT department of your company:

- The domain name of the office e-mail server
- Your work e-mail password
- The name of your exchange server

If the folks in IT are okay with you using your phone to access its e-mail service, your IT department will have no trouble supplying you with this information.

Before you set up your work e-mail on your phone, make sure that you have permission. If you do this without the green light from your company, and you end up violating your company's rules, you could be in hot water. Increasing your productivity won't be much help if you're standing out in the parking lot holding all the contents of your office in a cardboard box.

Assuming that your company wants you to be more productive with no extra cost to the company, the process for adding your work e-mail starts at your e-mail Home screen. In fact, all the steps are the same as the previous section up to Step 4, so use those steps and then come back here.

1. **Tap Manual Setup.**

   This brings up a screen that offers three choices: POP3 Account, IMAP Account, or Exchange Account. See these choices in Figure 6-7.

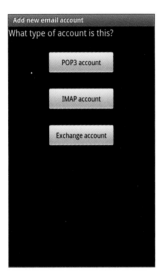

Figure 6-7: The menu pop-up for the Email app.

2. **Tap Exchange Account.**

   This brings up a screen like that shown in Figure 6-8. Some of the fields might be populated based upon the information that you enter at Step 5 in the preceding step list.

3. **Verify that information, and enter any missing data, according to what your IT department provided you.**

4. **Tap Next.**

   This begins synching with your work e-mail.

   Within a minute, you should start seeing your work e-mail messages appearing. If this doesn't happen, contact the IT department at your employer.

Figure 6-8: The manual set-up screen for adding corporate e-mail accounts.

Reading E-Mail on Your Phone

In Figure 6-7, you can see how the Home screen looks for e-mail when you have multiple e-mail accounts. At any given time, you might want to look at the accounts individually or all together. Taking either approach is quick and easy.

To look at all your e-mails in one large inbox, tap Combined Inbox. This lists all your e-mails in chronological order. To open any e-mail, just tap it.

If, on the other hand, you want to see just e-mails from one account, tap that account name to bring up your e-mails in chronological order for just that e-mail address.

The screen on your phone looks similar to when you had a single e-mail account. However, as shown in Figure 6-9, the screen is a little different.

Note the tab along the top, with the second account (Bill's MSN, in this case). To get to the next account, just tap its name.

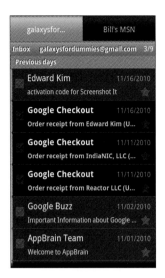

Figure 6-9: The Email screen when you have multiple accounts.

Writing and Sending an E-Mail

After you set up the receiving part of e-mail, the other important side is composing and sending e-mails. At any time when you're in an e-mail screen, simply tap the Menu button to get a pop-up screen.

There, tap the Compose icon shown in Figure 6-10.

Figure 6-10: The Compose icon on the Menu pop-up.

Here's the logic as to which e-mail account will be assigned to ultimately send this e-mail:

✔ If you're in the inbox of an e-mail account and you tap the Compose icon after tapping Menu, your phone will send the e-mail to the intended recipient(s) through that account.

✔ If you're in the combined inbox or some other part of the e-mail application, your phone will assume that you want to send the e-mail from the default e-mail account that you selected when you registered your second (or additional) e-mail account.

When you tap the Compose icon in the Menu pop-up, it tells you which account it will use. The Email composition screen in Figure 6-11 shows this e-mail will be coming from this account: galaxysfordummies@gmail.com.

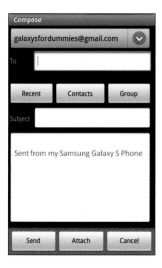

Figure 6-11: E-mail composition screen.

As shown in this screen, the top has a stalwart To field, where you type the address of the intended recipient. You can also call up your contacts, a group, or your most recent e-mail addresses. (Read all about contacts in Chapter 5.) You tap the address or contact you want, and it populates the To field.

Below that, in the Subject field, is where you enter the subject of the e-mail. And below that is the body of the e-mail, with the default signature, Sent from my Samsung Galaxy S phone, although this signature might have been customized for your cellular carrier.

At the bottom of the screen are three icons.

✔ **Send:** Tap this icon to send the e-mail to the intended recipient(s).

✔ **Attach:** Tap this to attach a file of any variety to your e-mail.

✔ **Cancel:** Tap this if you change your mind about sending an e-mail. If you're partially done with the message, you're asked whether you want to save it in your Drafts folder.

The Drafts folder (refer to the Email app Home screen in Figure 6-6) works like the Drafts folder in your computer's e-mail program. When you want to continue working on a saved e-mail, you open the Drafts folder, tap on it, and continue working.

Replying to or forwarding the e-mails that you get is a common activity. You can do this from your Email app. Figure 6-12 shows a typical e-mail that's opened.

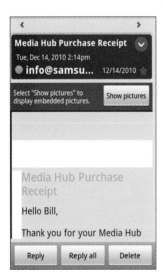

Figure 6-12: An opened e-mail.

You can Reply or Reply All by tapping the button visible at the bottom of the page. When you tap either of these options, the Reply screen comes back with the To line populated by the sender's e-mail address (or addresses) and a blank space where you can leave your comments.

To Forward the e-mail, tap the appropriate Menu option of the Device Function keys. After you tap Forward, you enter the addressee just like you do when sending a new e-mail.

Part III
Live on the Internet: Going Mobile

6:29pm, Nov 22 (8)

In this part . . .

The ability to access the Internet when you're away from your computer opens a new dimension of convenience, entertainment, and productivity. You don't want to have to lug around a laptop everywhere you go — and with a Samsung Galaxy S, you don't need to.

This part shows you how to get the most value out of the mobile Internet with as little hassle as possible. I tell you everything from how to access the mobile version of your favorite Web sites to how to buy new applications that run on your phone.

You've Got the Whole (Web) World in Your Hands

In This Chapter

▷ Surfing the Internet from your phone

▷ Setting the Browsing settings for you

▷ Visiting Web sites

*I*f you're like most people, one of the reasons you got a smartphone is because you want Internet access. You don't want to have to wait until you get back to your laptop or desktop to find the information you need online. You want to be able to access the Internet even when you're away from a Wi-Fi hotspot — and that's exactly what you can do with your Galaxy S phone. In this chapter, I show you how.

The browser that comes standard with your Galaxy S Phone works almost identically to the browser that's currently on your PC. You see many familiar tool-bars, including the Favorites and search engine. And the mobile version of the browser includes tabs that allow you to open multiple Internet sessions simultaneously.

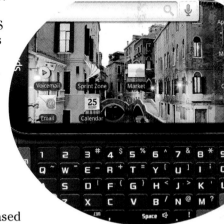

This chapter goes into much more detail on using the Internet browser on your Galaxy S Phone as well as the Web sites that you can access from your phone.

For what it's worth, the browser on your phone is based upon Google's Chrome browser but is designed to operate on a smaller screen.

Starting the Browser

To launch the browser on your Galaxy S phone, tap the Browser icon on one of the Home screens (shown in Figure 7-1). Alternatively, tap the Application icon and then tap the Browser icon.

Figure 7-1: The Browser icon.

As long as you're connected to the Internet (that is, either near a Wi-Fi hot-spot or in an area where you have cellular service), your home page appears. Your default home page could be blank, but most cellular carriers set their phones' home pages to their own Web sites or to a site selected by them.

If you're out of coverage range, or you turned off the cellular and Wi-Fi radios because you turned on Airplane mode, you'll get a pop-up screen letting you know that there is no Internet connection. (Read about Airplane mode in Chapter 2.)

If you should be in coverage but are not, or when you get off the airplane, you can reestablish your connections by pulling down the Notification screen and either tapping the Wi-Fi icon at the top and/or turning off Airplane mode.

Accessing Mobile (Or Not) Web Sites

After the browser is up, it's designed to function like the browser on your PC. At any time, you can enter a Web address (the URL) by tapping the text box at the top of the screen.

For example, the page seen in Figure 7-2 is the mobile version of the Web site RefDesk.com.

You can get to this site by entering **m.refdesk.com** into the text block at the top from the software keyboard.

As a comparison, Figure 7-3 shows the PC version of this site. It has many more pictures, and the text is smaller. The mobile version loads faster, but looks less flashy.

Figure 7-2: The mobile version of the Web site RefDesk.com.

Figure 7-3: The PC version of RefDesk.com.

RefDesk.com is far from the only Web site to offer a mobile version of its site. Many sites — everything from Facebook to Flickr, Gmail to Wikipedia — offer mobile versions.

So how do you get to the mobile Web sites? You don't have to worry about it! If a Web site has a mobile version, your phone browser will automatically bring it up. Samsung has gone out of its way to work to make the Web experience on the Galaxy S phone as familiar as possible to what you experience on your PC.

So that you know what you're looking for, the most common formats for addresses of mobilized Web sites are

- **Replacing the www with m:** For example, the mobile version of www. refdesk.com is m.refdesk.com.

- **Adding /mobile.com at the end of the address:** For example, the mobile version of Amazon.com is www.amazon.com/mobile.

When a site doesn't offer a mobile version or you just prefer to view the standard version of a particular site, you're not out of luck. Galaxy still allows you to view the full Web site. You have to stretch and pinch to find the information you need. (Stretch and pinch are hand movements you can use to enlarge/shrink what you see onscreen, as covered in Chapter 2.)

Setting the Default Browser Home Page

In most cases, your cellular carrier has set the default home page on the browser to access its Web site. And that's not just ego. There are valuable resources for you on that site to help you with access to customer service information.

On the other hand, maybe you just want the carrier's home page bookmarked but make another site your home page. From an open browser, the steps are as follows:

1. **Enter the Web address of the site you wish to make the home page.**

   Make sure that that page fully loads; give it a few moments.

2. **Tap the Menu button of the Device Function keys.**

   This brings up a pop-up screen like that shown in Figure 7-4.

3. **Tap the More icon.**

   This brings up a list of options.

Figure 7-4: Menu options for the browser.

4. **Tap the Settings hyperlink.**

   This brings up a long list of settings that you can control.

5. **Tap the Set Home Page link.**

   This brings up a pop-up screen that will populate the Web address you entered.

6. **Tap OK.**

   You have a new home page!

Navigating the Browser

With the browser active on your phone, tap the Menu key to open a menu showing several options, as shown in Figure 7-4.

- ✒ **New Window:** Tap to open a new tab — the equivalent to a new Web page.

- ✒ **Bookmarks:** Tap this icon to get access to all of your bookmarks. I talk more about bookmarks in the next section. *Note:* This icon is only on the menu pop-up for the Verizon Fascinate and the Sprint Epic 4G.

- ✒ **Windows:** Tap to bring up thumbnails of your open browser sessions. Read more on this subject later in this chapter.

- ✒ **Refresh:** Tap to resend data from the active tab. This is useful if there is no activity for a while.

- ✒ **Forward:** If you've used the Back button (one of the Device Function keys), tap Forward to logically move backward to an earlier screen. If you then want to get back to where you were, tap this button to move forward. If you haven't used the Back button, Forward is, of course, grayed out.

- ✒ **More:** Tap to bring up more options to control your browser, such as setting a new home page and making changes to font sizes.

Using Bookmarks

As convenient as it is to type URLs or search terms with the keyboard, you'll find it's usually faster to store a Web address that you visit frequently as a bookmark. Making bookmarks is a handy way to create a list of your favorite sites that you want to access over and over again.

The term "bookmarks" is roughly the equivalent of a Favorite on a Microsoft Internet Explorer browser.

In this section, I tell you how to bookmark a site and add it to your list of favorites. I also tell you how you can see your list of bookmarks.

Adding bookmarks

When you want to add a site to your bookmark list, simply visit the site. From there, follow these steps:

1. **Tap the Menu button of the Device Function keys.**

    This brings up a pop-up (refer to Figure 7-4).

2. **Tap the More icon.**

3. **From the list of options that appears, tap the Add Bookmark hyperlink.**

    This brings up a pop-up with a short name of the Web site on the top text box and the full address in the lower text box, as shown in Figure 7-5.

Figure 7-5: Add a Web site to your bookmarks.

4. Tap OK.

This URL is now in your bookmarks, as shown in Figure 7-6.

Figure 7-6: You can now access your URL from the Bookmarks page.

Getting to the bookmark screen

To use the sites that you've bookmarked, you need to get to the Bookmarks screen. The fastest way is to tap the button next to the address bar (it looks like a ribbon with a star).

An example of this is seen in Figure 7-7, on the RefDesk.com site.

Bookmark icon

Figure 7-7: The bookmark icon on
an open Web page.

When you tap the bookmark icon, you go to the list of all your bookmarks.
This is seen in either thumbnail view (refer to Figure 7-6) or list view, as
shown in Figure 7-8.

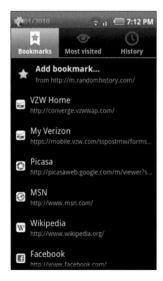

Figure 7-8: The Bookmarks page
as thumbnails or in list view.

Your phone will be set as default to one view type or the other. To change the view, simply tap the Menu button and select the other option.

Browsing to a site via a bookmark

The image in Figure 7-8 shows you a list of all your bookmarked sites. In addition, your phone probably came with a number of popular sites preloaded on your phone. The preloaded sites are grayed out until you use them.

To open a site, all you need to do is tap the thumbnail image (in thumbnail view) or hyperlink name (in list view).

When you open the Bookmarks page for the first time, the screen has several popular Web sites that are grayed out. The first time that you tap them, they will appear in color. This is done for your convenience. You can keep them or discard them as you want.

Bookmark housekeeping

Press and hold a thumbnail on the bookmarks list to bring up the following options presented in Figure 7-9:

Reference, Facts, News - Fre... http://www.refdesk.com/
Open
Open in new window
Edit bookmark
Add shortcut to Home
Share link
Copy link URL
Delete bookmark
Set as homepage

Figure 7-9: Bookmark options.

✓ **Open:** This option does the same as tapping a bookmark thumbnail.

✓ **Open in New Window:** Tapping this icon opens the bookmarked Web site but in another tab. I cover managing tabs in the later section, "Navigating Multiple Browser Sessions."

✓ **Edit Bookmark:** Tap to change the Web address (URL) of the site that you bookmarked.

✓ **Add Shortcut to Home:** Tap to put the thumbnail of this site on your extended Home screen.

✓ **Share Link:** Tap to send this Web address to a friend through e-mail or MMS.

✓ **Copy Link URL:** Tap to copy the address of the Web site for use in another application.

✓ **Delete Bookmark:** Tap to remove this Web site from your bookmark list.

✓ **Set as Homepage:** Tap to replace the existing home page — the Web site that opens when you first bring up your browser — with this Web site.

Putting a Web site on your Home screen

In addition to using bookmarks, you can also put a link on your phone's Home screen. This will result in even faster access to your favorite Web sites.

To put a site on the Home screen of the phone, it must first be stored as a bookmark. From within the bookmark screen, you bring up the Bookmark options as described in the previous section.

Tap the Add Shortcut to Home link. This puts an icon for the Web site on the Home screen of your phone.

Your history on display

In Figure 7-8, on the Bookmarks page, the screen opens to the thumbnails of your bookmarked Web sites. Along the top are two other options:

✓ **Most Visited:** This list keeps track of the sites that you've ever viewed. This is shown in Figure 7-10.

✓ **History:** The History list, shown in Figure 7-11, is a list of the Web sites you've viewed, most recently, in reverse chronological order.

Accessing your History list is another way of getting to your Favorites without adding them to your Bookmarks. This is useful if you need to access that particular Web site for only a short period of time.

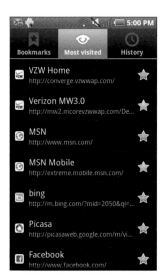

Figure 7-10: See your most-visited Web sites.

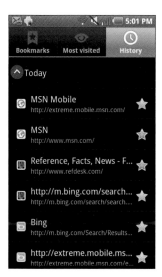

Figure 7-11: Your viewing history.

To remove any entry from your History list, press and hold the thumbnail and then tap Remove from History.

Navigating Multiple Browser Sessions

As I mention earlier, it can be convenient to open multiple browser sessions — called *windows* or *tabs* — at the same time. Each window is open to its own Web site. You can jump around each session with ease without the need for a new site to load each time.

To jump among the windows, you must access the Windows screen. You do this from an existing browser session.

1. **Tap the Menu button of the Device Function keys.**

   This brings up a pop-up screen (refer to Figure 7-4).

2. **Tap the Windows icon.**

   This brings up the screen of open browser sessions, as shown in Figure 7-12.

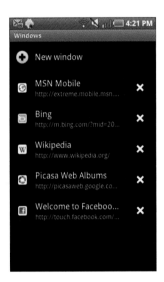

Figure 7-12: The Windows screen to manage multiple browser sessions.

Figure 7-12 shows list view. If you prefer thumbnail view, tap the Menu button and then tap that option.

You go to the desired session by tapping the image. You return to the open windows by tapping the Menu button and tapping Windows. It doesn't get any easier than this.

To keep it straight, you can open a new window a number of ways:

- **From an existing browser session:** Tap the Menu button of the Device Function keys. This brings up the pop-up menu shown in Figure 7-4. Then tap New Window.

- **From within Bookmarks, Recently Viewed, or History:** Press and hold one of the Web sites. This brings up the options shown in Figure 7-9. Then tap the Open in New Window link.

- **From the Windows screen (refer to Figure 7-12):** Tap the New Window link on the line above the open sessions.

Googling Your Way to the Information You Need: Mobile Google Searches

When you open the browser, you can use any search engine that you want (for example, Bing or Yahoo!). Still, some functions — Web searches and map searches — work especially well when you use the Google search engine.

At the highest level, the search process works just like on your PC: You type (or tap) in a search topic, press Enter, and the search engine goes and finds it. Depending upon the search engine and your phone, you might even have the ability to speak your search topic (search by voice).

Android works well with the Google browser primarily because Android was developed by Google.

The Galaxy S phone works to make Internet searches more convenient. You can tap the Search button on the front of the phone and begin a search. There is no need to bring up a browser to open a search engine and then enter your inquiry. Just tap the Home button (if necessary) and then the Search button (a Device Function key), as shown in Figure 7-13, to get the same results.

Figure 7-13: The Search icon on your browser.

The Search button is sensitive to the context of what's onscreen. For example, if you're on a map search, it'll assume that you're searching for a location. When you're at the Home screen, pressing the Search button will do a general Internet search.

If you want to avoid having to be concerned that the Search button will limit itself to a location, you can always press the Home button first and then press the Search button.

Exploring Widgets and Applications

In This Chapter

▶ Managing preloaded widgets

▶ Discovering preloaded apps

▶ Using the clock and alarm widgets

*T*his chapter covers the software that comes with your phone out of the box. The kinds of software you can use fall into three categories:

✐ **Widgets:** Although "widget" can mean different things for different people, for this book, just know that a widget is a smallish application that takes care of a specific task. And, widgets are almost always free.

Your phone comes with several preloaded widgets, such as a calculator, and also a memo widget (for simple note taking).

✐ **Games:** These software applications are for entertainment.

✐ **Applications:** "Applications" include everything else, such as software packages that provide useful information or offer convenience. They can be free, or they can be for-fee. In any case, they're available to you to address a long list of problems — some that you probably didn't even know that you had!

In this chapter, I fill you in on the widgets and apps already on your phone but that might need authorization (from you) to use.

Checking Out the Preloaded Widgets

Your phone comes with dozens of preloaded widgets; some are from Samsung, and others are selected by your cellular carrier. Samsung and/or your carrier could have activated them, but there is a great deal of overlap among them. It would have been repetitive redundancy over and over again.

The compromise is to make the preloads readily available but let you go through and pick which ones you like the best. Yeah, this is a little more work on your part, but if you want to have seven variations of a clock on your extended Home screen, have at it. Don't say that Samsung didn't give you a choice in the matter.

Here's how to check out the preloaded widgets on your phone. Start at the Home screen. Then follow these simple steps:

1. **From the extended Home screen, tap the Menu button.**

2. **From the menu that opens (see Figure 8-1), tap the Add button.**

   The menu shown in Figure 8-2 appears.

Figure 8-1: The Menu pop-up button from the Home screen.

Figure 8-2: This menu includes widgets from Samsung and your carrier.

3. Tap either Samsung Widgets or Android Widgets.

To arrive at the screen shown in Figure 8-3, I first opted for Samsung. (I discuss other good Android widgets later. Take a look.)

Figure 8-3: The Samsung widgets.

The Samsung widgets

Samsung preloads some widgets on all of its phones, including the following.

✔ **Buddies Now:** Takes messages from your top friends and brings them together in one spot, which makes keeping in touch with comments from your friends easier. A buddy is someone in your contacts list.

✔ **Calendar Clock:** Posts an analog-looking clock with the date on the extended Home page.

✔ **Daily Briefing:** Brings together weather, financial news, national news, and any calendar appointments in one screen of your extended Home page. These subjects are updated regularly. A sample of a Daily Briefing page is shown in Figure 8-4. This widget encompasses so many things I've devoted Chapter 16 to it.

Figure 8-4: A sample of a Daily Briefing page.

✔ **Days Widget:** Allows you to create a diary in which you can add images, text, and your schedule. It also has a link to weather reports.

✔ **Dual Clock:** Puts up a digital clock and a second clock based upon a location that you set. This is like a world clock that tells your time, and the local time of a place in which you are interested.

✔ **Feeds and Updates:** Collects updates from multiple social networking and business sites, such as Facebook and your e-mail account, and alerts you to updates.

✔ **Y! Finance Clock:** Puts up an analog clock with a hyperlink to a ticker symbol of interest to you. When you tap the name of the stock, the screen takes you to the latest price, delayed by 15 minutes.

✔ **Program Monitor:** Tells you the status of applications that are up and running.

As you might have noticed, several widgets are available to display the current time. By loading these on the phone — but not launching them all — Samsung gives you the choice of what you want to display.

When you see a widget that you like (or two, or three), all you do is tap on it. The widget is placed on your Home screen and added to your Application list.

The Android widgets

In addition to the Samsung widgets, your Galaxy S sports a number of pre-loaded Android widgets although these have been specified by your wireless carrier, and vary by phone.

Android widgets include the following, but note that this is just a partial list of what might be on your phone. There might be more or less widgets on your particular phone model.

✔ **Picture Frame:** Takes an image and puts it inside a picture frame on your extended Home page.

✔ **Power Control:** Gives you access on your Home screen to adjust the settings of the largest users of battery life on your phone. These include options such as your radios (Wi-Fi and Bluetooth) and the screen brightness.

✔ **YouTube:** Puts a hyperlink on your Home screen that takes you to the mobile version of Google's YouTube service.

✔ **Facebook:** Puts a hyperlink on your Home screen that takes you to the mobile version of Facebook.

When you enter your e-mail address and password into this widget, it's difficult to change. If you let someone use your phone, make sure that they don't get to the Facebook Widget and enter their Facebook account information before you do!

✔ **Latitude:** An application developed by Google that gives others permission to know your location. This feature is convenient, say, if you want to meet up with family members at a large mall or an amusement park.

✔ **WeatherBug:** A service that gives you information on weather based upon numerous local weather stations. A slick additional feature with WeatherBug is that it displays the local outside temperature on the notification bar at the very top of the screen. The notification bar has the icons that tell you information like signal strength, if you have any unread email text, or if you need to take some action.

Widgets, like some applications, can come as free but have a version that has a fee. The version that you pay for will offer some additional capability, come without advertising, or both. If the additional capability isn't of interest and the advertising doesn't bother you, stick with the free version.

If any of these widgets strike your fancy, but aren't preloaded on your phone for some reason, chances are that they'd be available from Android Market or other Android Web sites. Chapter 9 describes this process for finding them.

Adding and deleting widgets from your Home screen

Each widget, whether preloaded or one that you download, is listed on the Application list. Tapping the Applications icon brings you to the list of all applications, in alphabetic order.

To me, maintaining a list like this with 50 icons is manageable. To you, maybe a list with 100 icons is acceptable. It's up to you. The Application list will grow as big as you need. However, it can become so big that it's virtually unusable. Be aware of this possibility when you're adding widgets and applications like crazy.

Preloaded widgets are automatically placed on your extended Home page when you activate them. This is different from when you add applications.

To remove any widget (or for that matter, application) from the extended Home screen, simply press and hold on that icon. In about a second, a garbage can icon will appear at the bottom of the screen, as shown in Figure 8-5.

Simply drag the widget or application icon to the garbage icon, and it will be, for all practical purposes, deleted. If you change your mind and want it back, you can re-add it by following the instructions for adding a widget earlier in this chapter.

Deleting an icon from the Home screen does not delete the application from the phone. It remains in the App list. If you would like to actually uninstall the widget, see Chapter 9.

Figure 8-5: Deleting a widget from your phone.

 You can delete any application you have downloaded from your phone. It is a different matter to delete an application that came preloaded. An advanced user may be able to do this, but if you don't know what you're doing, you may delete some files that are needed by other apps. It is best to learn to live with the apps that came with your phone.

Extended Home Screen Apps: The Tip-Top Taps

The applications accessible from the extended Home screen include the following. These applications are the ones that Samsung determined to be the top priority for most Galaxy S Phone users. Your cellular carrier might customize this screen by reprioritizing or adding more applications that it sees as important. In any case, you launch the app by tapping it.

- **Browser:** The mobile version of the Web browser that's familiar to PC users. More on this in Chapter 7.

- **Market:** Takes you to the Android Market. Chapter 9 discusses how to get the most from this service.

- **Camera:** Launches the phone's camera, with which you can take high resolution pictures and shoot digital video.

✔ **Gallery:** Allows you to sort the still images on your phone, including the ones that you have taken with the camera as well as others that you've downloaded. Chapter 10 explores how to get the most out of the Camera and the Gallery applications.

✔ **Email:** Your Galaxy S brings together on this one application up to ten e-mail services. Read more about this capability in Chapter 6.

✔ **Maps:** A mapping application that (when enabled), can show your location on a map. And you can get real-time directions to a location. The steps to make this happen are in Chapter 12.

✔ **Calendar:** Store events and be alerted as their times approach. Chapter 14 covers the Calendar app in detail.

The applications on the Home screen are the easiest to access. However, by tapping the Application icon (of the Device Function keys), you can see all the applications that are on your phone.

If you want to add an icon to launch an application from the extended Home screen, press and hold the icon on the Application list, and a copy of that icon will appear on the last Home screen that you had open.

To make an icon on the extended Home screen go away and appear only on the Application list, press and hold the icon on the Home screen. In a second, a garbage can icon will show up on the bottom. Simply drag the icon to the garbage can. It will turn red for a second and then disappear from your Home screen although it does remain on your Application list.

You can navigate to all your applications by flicking the screen to the right or left.

Even if you just bought your Galaxy S phone, the list of applications is extensive, and it'll grow as you add more applications. I talk about adding applications in Chapter 9. Figure 8-6 shows a typical Application list. Your phone, of course, will have its own list of applications.

The applications that are accessible from the Application list include (but are not limited to) the following:

✔ **Clock:** There are already enough widgets for displaying the time on your Home screen! From this application, you can set an alarm, quickly view a series of clocks set for remote cities, use a stopwatch, and set a countdown timer. The next section goes into how to set these options.

✔ **Calculator:** This app (shown in Figure 8-7) is a straightforward algebraic calculator. And that's pretty much all there is to say about it.

Figure 8-6: All the applications on your phone are just a flick away.

Figure 8-7: The calculator. Go figure.

> ✔ **Memo:** This basic word processing application stores documents on your phone. If you ever want to send this document to someone, you can e-mail the document as an attachment. The receiving end has to know how to handle a .vnt file, however, which is pretty much exactly what other Android phones know how to do.

> ✔ **Settings:** Make a number of adjustments to the default settings on your phone.

Setting grid or list view

The two ways to view the apps in your App list are as a grid (the default) or as a vertical list. Both options are shown in Figure 8-8.

Figure 8-8: Grid (left) and list view (right) of your apps.

There is no right or wrong option. Pick the one that works for you.

You set your preference when you're in the App list. When you tap the Menu button, you get the option to toggle to the other format. How this works depends on the version of your phone. The menu offers you two options:

> ✔ Toggle between grid and list views.

> ✔ A View Type option. Tap that to bring up a pop-up with the three options:

- Customizable grid
- Alphabetical grid
- Alphabetical list

Select your option by tapping it. Done.

Changing the order of your apps

You can customize the grid layout. Depending upon the model of your Galaxy S phone, there are two ways to customize your Grid layout while in the App list.

1. **Tap Menu, of the Device Function keys.**

2. **Tap the Edit icon on the pop-up.**

   If you don't see the Edit option, select View Type and then choose Customizable Grid. Now tap the menu, and you'll see the Edit option.

Figure 8-9 shows a regular grid next to a customizable grid ready to be changed.

Figure 8-9: The default grid view (left) and customizable grid (right).

When customizable, grid icons have a white outline visible on the upper-left corner of each icon. You can move them if you press and hold on them. Then you can drag them where you want.

Icons sporting a red circle with a white horizontal line are applications that you've added since you acquired the phone. In Figure 8-9, the Amazon MP3 is such an app.

Using Clock Functions and Setting Alarms

As mentioned, the Clock application includes four functions:

- Alarm
- World Clock
- Stopwatch
- Timer

Alarm

The Alarm application allows you to set a time for a signal to go off. If you want to keep it simple and just set an alarm once, you can use the default settings.

Before you get started, you want to know at least the following:

- The time you want the alarm to sound
- Whether you want it to ring once or multiple times
- The alarm volume

The phone will do its job, and alert you once. Here's how to set up an alarm for the Verizon Fascinate, the AT&T Captivate, and the T-Mobile Vibrant. In a bit, I talk about setting the alarm for the Sprint Epic 4G.

1. **From the Application list, find the Clock (or Alarm & Clocks) app and tap it.**

   This brings up Figure 8-10.

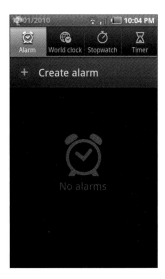

Figure 8-10: The Clock screen.

2. **From the Clock screen, tap Create Alarm.**

   This brings up Figure 8-11. Because it has many choices, this image is taller than one screen. On your phone, Figure 8-11 covers several screen heights. Just move the screen to get them all.

3. **Set the alarm at the time you want and then tap Save.**

   If you take the default settings, the alarm will signal once.

   At the appointed time, you will get a screen. An example is shown in Figure 8-12, although each phone is a little different.

To turn off the alarm, depending upon your phone, you either press and hold the red button on the alert screen, slide the red button, or tap Dismiss.

The alarm clock for the Epic 4G is simpler than the Create Alarm screens for the other Galaxy versions. It comes with three preset alarms that are not activated. You simply edit the existing alarms with the time, and off you go!

The Epic 4G also doesn't have the World Clock, Stopwatch, and Timer apps. All these are downloadable as widgets from Android Market, though.

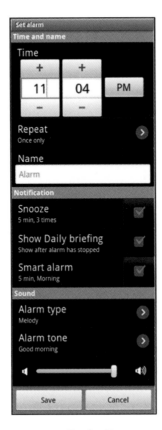

Figure 8-11: The Set Alarm screen.

You can set many other options to make the alarm more convenient. Or, if you want to get more sophisticated, you can set the alarm to go off at the same time every day, or to change the alarm sound.

Before you create an alarm, I recommend having the following choices in mind:

- **A descriptive name for the alarm:** Think of something clear, such as *Morning Wake Up* or *Get the Kids from Daycare.*

- **How often the alarm should sound:** The default is once, but you can set it for the same time every day, during weekdays, or even selected days, like Tuesdays and Thursdays.

Figure 8-12: A typical alarm alert screen.

- ✔ **To snooze or not to snooze:** Set whether you want to allow a "snooze" option where the alarm alerts you once, and then alerts you again a few minutes later — and if so, how much later and how many times before it gives up on you.

- ✔ **Soft awakening:** Set whether you want to have the phone wait until you are done with your last dream. I am not making this up. This capability is called Smart Alarm, and I talk more about this later.

- ✔ **The alarm sound, if any:** You can have an alarm that just vibrates. Or, you can have an alarm that vibrates and chimes, beeps, chirps, makes noises like a babbling book, plays your favorite song, or reads you the Gettysburg Address.

To get what you want, follow these steps:

1. **From the Set Alarm screen (refer to Figure 8-11), tap Repeat.**

   The Alarm Repeat screen opens, as shown in Figure 8-13. The default is Once Only.

2. **(Optional) Set the alarm for every day, weekdays, or specific days of the week. To set the days of the week**

   a. Tap Weekly.

   b. Then tap the days of the week when you want the alarm.

   They turn blue when enabled.

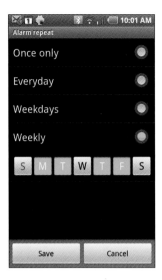

Figure 8-13: The Alarm Repeat options.

3. Tap Save.

This brings you back to the Set Alarm screen.

4. Tap in the text box under Name to give this alarm a name.

On the onscreen keyboard that pops up, type a name you can remember. Then tap Save.

5. Select the type of notification — that is, whether to set up the snooze option, have the Daily Briefing feature start updating when the alarm goes off, and enable the Smart Alarm.

- *Snooze:* The Snooze function is a familiar option for most of us (some more than others). Tap this option to set how long Snooze is supposed to wait between rings and how many times before it gives up. Tap Save. Done.

- *Daily Briefing:* To have the Daily Briefing update at alarm time, tap the check box. Or not, as you prefer.

- *Smart Alarm:* Smart Alarm is more complicated. I explain it in more detail later in this chapter.

6. Tap the Alarm Type.

This can be just a melody, just a vibration, both a vibration and a melody, or a voice. Figure 8-14 presents the screen.

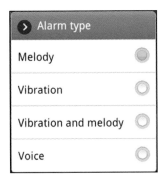

Figure 8-14: The Alarm Type choices.

Make your choice by tapping the description you want; it's automatically saved.

The Voice option is a bit more complicated. You'll be prompted to download a text-to-speech app because you probably don't have it. When enabled, Voice will read you the time of the alarm in addition to playing tones.

7. Select the Alarm Tone.

You get two choices: Sounds or Go to My Files, as shown in Figure 8-15.

Figure 8-15: Set an alarm tone.

You can listen to the pre-installed choices for tones to decide which option is sufficiently annoying, but not too obnoxious, for you. There is a wide variety of options.

If you opt for Go to My Files, you can select any sound or music file that's licensed for your phone. It could be your favorite music, or it could be the Gettysburg Address. What you play is your choice.

8. Set the Alarm volume.

Use the green slider bar at the bottom to set the volume for the alarm.

9. Tap Save.

The alarm name appears on the screen shown in Figure 8-11. To change the settings of an alarm that's already saved, all you need to do is tap on the alarm, and adjust the settings.

The goal of the Smart Alarm is to wake you gently after you finish your last dream of the night. This sounds lovely, but it takes a little getting used to — as well as needing some faith.

First, the way this works is that you put the phone in bed next to you. The phone calculates when you're coming out of a dream stage, based upon an analysis of your movements in the bed.

If you place the phone next to your bed, or it falls on the floor, it won't sense your movements. In this case, the Smart Alarm won't work as planned.

When Smart Alarm approaches the time of the alarm setting, it will judge where you are in your sleep cycle. When it determines that you finished your last dream, it will start playing a "soothing tone" of your choice, such as Rain or Breeze. These ramp up slowly so that it doesn't startle you as you awake from your slumber.

When you check the option to use Smart Alarm, it asks you the duration and tone that you prefer. Set these and then tap Save.

I recommend that you go ahead and set a regular alarm with the loud, obnoxious type of sound as a backup plan. It would be nice to awake gently, but it's not worth it if you get in trouble for being late to work.

World Clock

The World Clock function allows you to see the local time for a number of cities. An example of this is shown in Figure 8-16, populated with Seattle and Chicago.

You can choose from an extensive list of cities. The process to add a new city is straightforward.

Set your home location first. It makes comparison to the other cities easier.

1. From the World Clock screen shown in Figure 8-16, tap Add City.

A long list of major metro areas appears. You can flick down to the city you want or you can start typing in the Search Cities text box.

2. **Tap the city that you want.**

   A clock with the local time of that city appears on the World Clock screen.

Figure 8-16: View times around the world.

To delete a city, just press and hold on the name of the city. A pop-up screen will ask you what you want to do. Select Delete.

Be sure to set the appropriate daylight savings setting for the city you select. Add this by tapping on the Menu icon and then tapping DST settings.

Stopwatch

The Stopwatch screen is shown in on the left in Figure 8-17. You start the clock by tapping the green button. When the stopwatch is running, you can tap Stop to get a time, or Lap to get a split time (shown on the right in Figure 8-17). When you stop, you can either clear the time or restart where you left off.

Timer

The Timer counts down time. To set the amount of time to count down, you select the hours, minutes, and seconds, as shown in Figure 8-18. When Timer reaches all zeroes, it vibrates and plays a tone. You must press and hold the red X to stop the alarm. There is not a way to change this alarm.

Figure 8-17: Time events with the stopwatch.

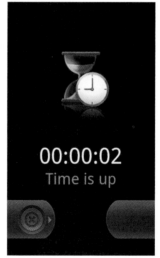

Figure 8-18: Timer alarm screen.

Downloading Apps from Android Market

In This Chapter

▷ Getting to know Android Market

▷ Finding Android Market on your phone

▷ Seeing what Android Market has to offer

▷ Downloading apps from Android Market

*O*ne of the things that makes smartphones (like the phones based upon the Google Android platform) different from regular cellphones is that you can download better applications than what comes standard on the phone. Most traditional cellphones come with a few simple games and basic applications. Smartphones come with better games and applications. For example, on your Galaxy S phone, you get a more sophisticated Contact Manager, an application that can play digital music (MP3s), basic maps, and texting tools.

To boot, you can get even better applications and games for phones based on the Google Android platform. Numerous applications are available for your Galaxy S phone, and that number will certainly grow over time.

So, where do you get all these wonderful applications? The primary place to get Android apps is the Android Market. You might be happy with the applications that came with your Galaxy S phone, but look into the Android Market, and you'll find apps you suddenly won't be able to live without.

In this chapter, I introduce you to the Android Market and give you a taste of what you find there. I then show you how to find and download applications.

The Android Market: The Mall for Your Phone

The Android Market is set up and run by Google to provide applications for people with Android phones. Adding an application to your phone is similar to adding software to your PC. In both cases, a new application (or software) makes you more productive, adds to your convenience, and entertains you for hours on end — sometimes for free. Not a bad deal.

There are some important differences, however, between installing software on a PC and getting an application on a cellphone:

✔ **Smartphone applications need to be more stable than computer software because of their greater potential for harm.** If you buy an application for your PC and find that it's unstable (for example, it causes your PC to crash), sure, you'll be upset. If you were to acquire an unstable application for your phone, though, you could run up a huge phone bill or even take down the regional cellphone network. Can you hear me now?

✔ **There are multiple smartphone platforms.** These days, it's pretty safe to assume that computer software will run on a PC or a Mac or both. On the other hand, because of the various smartphone platforms out there, different versions within a given platform aren't always compatible. The Android Market ensures that the application you're buying will work with your version of phone.

Unlike the Apple App Store and the Windows Phone Marketplace, Google takes much more of a hands-off approach to letting applications into the Android Market. This is attractive to many developers who bristle at the thought of censorship. The expectation is that readily available feedback and market forces will force out any unstable applications. The good news for you as a user is that this policy attracts more daring applications developers. The bad news is that you might be the unlucky one to find out that the application you downloaded is unstable, or worse. I talk more about how to do your due diligence so you can confidently buy apps later in this chapter, in the "Being Wise about Widgets and Apps."

Getting to the Market

The easiest way to access the Android Market is through the Market application on your Galaxy S phone.

Chances are that there will be a shortcut to the Market on your Home screen, as shown in Figure 9-1.

Figure 9-1: The Android
Market icon.

If the Market application icon isn't already on your Home screen, you can find it in your Application list. To open it, simply tap the icon. You'll be greeted by the screen shown in Figure 9-2.

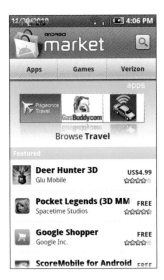

Figure 9-2: The Market home page.

As new applications become available, the applications in the Featured section will change, and the home page will change from one day to the next, but the categories will be consistent over time. These categories are

- ✔ **Apps:** These are applications that offer you convenience, information access or sorting, entertainment, or personal productivity.

- ✔ **Games:** These apps are for fun and enjoyment. As it happens, these are the most-downloaded kind of applications. Popularity is a good initial indication that the application is worth considering.

Throughout this book, I use the blanket term *applications* to refer to games and other kinds of applications. Some purists make a distinction between applications and games. The thing is, from the perspective of a phone user, they're the same. You download an application and use it, either for fun or to be more productive.

✔ **Carrier:** The third tab on the right is a special section supported by your carrier. In Figure 9-2, that's Verizon. This tab includes applications that your carrier has found to help you get more out of your ownership of your Galaxy S phone or achieve better service.

Signing up for a Gmail account

You probably have an e-mail account. In fact, you might have several. But if you're going to download and shop from the Android Market, you need one more account: one on Gmail. If you don't have one already, you'll be prompted to create a new account for your phone when you first access the Android Market from your phone.

This isn't cumbersome, and it opens many valuable services for your phone that I cover in subsequent chapters, including sharing photos, securely storing financial information, and making management of your contact list much more convenient.

Being Wise about Widgets and Apps

Take a minute to review the following important considerations before enabling any widget or any new application on your phone:

✔ **Security:** Before you load any applications on your phone, be aware of the possible threats, some of which aren't present in cellular phones that have lesser capabilities.

✔ **Space:** Your phone has a limited amount of space for you to download widgets and applications before things become unmanageable. I'm talking about adding so many widgets and apps that your Applications list becomes unwieldy, not memory.

✔ **Quality of the application:** There are no guarantees on the quality of the widget or application that you download to your phone.

Each of these considerations warrants further discussion.

Keeping an eye on security

When Google created the Android platform environment, it made the decision to make the platform wide open for applications developers. Unlike the development environments for the iPhone, the Windows Phone, and the BlackBerry OS, no governing organization is in place to authorize or approve an application. No one within Google or Android Market thoroughly verifies to make sure that application does exactly what it says — or does *more* than what it says, like potentially cause problems. This is mostly left to customer feedback.

You need to be very aware, therefore, of two kinds of threats that can (at least theoretically) be problematic when you use or acquire a new application or widget:

- **Data security:** A regular cellphone user might have only names and telephone numbers stored on his phone. You, however, might have every password that you use on the Internet stored somewhere on your phone. This includes all your e-mail accounts, credit card information, and even your bank accounts.

- **Your physical safety:** Your phone has precise information on where you are at every moment, and most applications use these data to make your life more convenient and safe. For example, I use mapping on phones to know whether my teenagers are generally where they say they are. My family also uses this technology to find each other at a crowded mall. However, the opposite can be true. If a villain can gain access to where you are, he can cause you harm.

This said, if a smartphone application was being used to rob people (like siphoning off personal information), you would have heard about a case or two. In practice, the following mechanisms can protect you:

- The skill and professionalism of the programmers to protect their customers

- The self-interest of the owners of the applications who see that protecting the reputation of their applications is good business

- User ratings on the application functions

Always look for the standardized warning that tells you what personal information is accessed by the application before you enable it on your phone. Figure 9-3 shows an example of such a warning that lists the resources to which the application has access. Like with any standard Warning dialog box, before you can proceed, you must acknowledge that you're okay with it.

Figure 9-3: Read the warnings when loading an application.

Here, however, is where the issue of human nature comes into play. How many of us actually pay attention to or read warnings? Many folks will just tap the OK button to proceed because they want the application, assuming that if there were a problem, others would have found it.

This then takes you back to relying on the integrity of the system. At the same time, the reality is that no system is perfectly safe and secure. Do not believe anyone that tells you otherwise.

If relying on the comments of others and the self-interest of manufacturers to put quality control on their products don't convince you that the convenience of using your phone is a manageable risk, you can get antivirus applications to protect your phone. I talk more about antivirus applications in Chapter 17. I recommend that you use one.

Monitoring space on your phone

Although they don't take up a lot of space individually, adding widgets and apps will eat some memory and take up space. So, when adding widgets and apps, just keep in mind your total memory demands, including files, applications, and games. Two factors limit the number of files, applications, and games you can add to your phone:

✔ How much memory storage for applications that reside on your phone

✔ How many widgets and apps you have to manage

Rest assured that you have plenty of room on your phone to store applications. And if you go a little wild and add lots of widgets, games, applications, and multimedia files, you can always add a storage card or get a larger one for not a lot of cash. The size of these cards is so large that you should never have to worry about running out of storage.

Having said that, the practical reality is that each widget and app adds an icon to your Application list, so you can see how adding lots of icons could get cumbersome. Adding 10, 20, or even 30 icons isn't that bad. However, some people go nuts adding files. Some find adding files to be addictive, particularly free ones.

Assessing widget and app quality

The greatest unknown is whether a widget or app will meet your expectations. One way is to load it and give it a try. Especially if it was free. If you don't like it, delete it. (I show you how, later in the chapter.) You wasted but a few minutes of your time.

Another option is to do your research before you take the time to download. Read about the widget or app online at Android Market; I show you later how to find this information. As a rule, look for widgets and apps with rankings higher than 3, that have tens of thousands of downloads or are very recent releases, and that come from a manufacturer that sounds familiar.

The app description at Android Market offers the basics you'd expect, such as title (name), price, feature highlights, and reviews. You can see a sample in Figure 9-4. You'll also find the following:

✔ **Application requirements:** Any special considerations that might be useful to know before acquiring the application. For example, an application might require another app to perform its functions.

✔ **Release date:** This is the official date this version came on the market.

✔ **Version:** This lets you compare the version you have with an updated release.

✔ **Company contact information:** This is the Web address and the contact for customer service questions.

✔ **Screenshot:** A representative image of the widget and application in use.

Figure 9-4: Read widget and app descriptions.

The customer service information is useful after you download the application. The release date and version information is of most use if you already have experience with this particular widget or app. That will come with time.

Deciding whether to download

With all the issues with concerns and issues discussed about widgets and apps, you might wonder why you should even bother. Well, because widgets and applications can do fun and exciting things for you!

Think of the inherent risks you face every time you get on your computer at home. There are many threats online that you shouldn't ignore. The expectation is that, if you're even moderately careful and vigilant to news on scams, you'll avoid most problems. The only sure way to avoid any risk is to pitch your PC into a recycling bin. After all, most of us are willing to take some risk to get the benefit of having a computer.

The risks associated with your Galaxy S — or any other smartphone — are similar to the threats on your PC. Before too long, you'll have loaded account names, passwords, and credit card information.

And just like on your PC, the authors of applications are very aware of this, going to great lengths to protect you and your information. At the same time, people can undermine these safeguards, usually to gain a little convenience. Don't be that person. Just be aware that the information on your Galaxy S is like your PC, and not like your old basic cellphone that only has your telephone numbers and pictures.

An additional consideration with your Galaxy S phone is that it knows where you are. You may be worried that stalkers could intercept this information and use it to track you when you are away from home, making you more vulnerable. Many applications that share your location information will warn you about this potential and go to extra lengths to make sure that someone other than the 911 operator can know where you are.

What's Available: Shopping for Android Apps

When you head to the local mall with a credit card but without a plan, you're asking for trouble. Anything and everything that tickles your fancy is fair game. Similarly, before you head to the Market, it helps if you have a sense what you're looking for, so you don't spend more than you intended.

The applications for your Galaxy S phone fall into the following subcategories:

- **Games:** Your Galaxy S phone takes interactive gaming to a new level. Games categories are explored in much more detail in Chapter 11.

- **Applications:** The "non-games" fall into many subcategories:

  - *Comics:* These are applications that are meant to be funny. Hopefully, you find something that tickles your funny bone.

  - *Communication:* Yes, the Galaxy S phone comes with many communications applications, but these Market apps enhance what comes with the phone: for example, tools that automatically send a message if you're running late to a meeting, or that text you if your kids leave a defined area.

  - *Entertainment:* Not games per se, but these apps are still fun: trivia, horoscopes, and frivolous noise-making apps. (These also include Chuck Norris "facts." Did you know that Chuck Norris can divide by 0?)

  - *Finance:* This is the place to find mobile banking applications and tools to make managing your personal finances easier.

  - *Health:* This is a category for all applications related to mobile medical applications, including calorie counters, fitness tracking, and tools that help manage chronic conditions, such as diabetes.

- *Lifestyle:* This category is a catch-all for applications that involve recreation or specials interests, like philately or bird watching.

- *Maps & Search:* Many applications tell you where you are and where you want to go. Some are updated with current conditions, and others are based upon static maps that use typical travel times.

- *Multimedia:* The Galaxy S phone comes with the music and video service, but nothing says you have to like them. You might prefer offerings that are set up differently or have a selection of music that isn't available elsewhere.

- *News & Weather:* You find a variety of apps that allow you to drill down into getting just the news or weather that is more relevant to you than what's available on your extended Home screen.

- *Productivity:* These apps are for money management (like a tip calculator), voice recording (like a stand-alone voice recorder), and time management (for example, an electronic to-do list).

- *Reference:* These apps include a range of reference books, such as dictionaries and translation guides. Think of this like the reference section of your local library and bookstore.

- *Shopping:* These applications help you with rapid access to mobile shopping sites or do automated comparison shopping.

- *Social:* These are the social networking sites. If you think that you know them all, check here. Of course, you'll find Facebook, LinkedIn, Twitter, and My Space, but there are dozens of other sites that are more narrowly focused that offer applications for the convenience of their users.

- *Sports:* Sports sites of all genres can be found in this part of the Market to tell you the latest scores and analysis.

- *Themes:* Your phone comes with color schemes or "themes." This part of the market offers a broader selection.

- *Tools:* Some of these are widgets that help you with some fun capabilities. Others are more complicated, and help you get more functionality from your phone.

- *Travel:* These apps are useful for traveling, such as currency translations and travel guides.

- *Demo:* These are small, sometimes frivolous, applications that are in this catch-all category for those applications that don't quite fit anywhere else.

- *Software Libraries:* Computers of all sizes come with software libraries to take care of special functions, such as tools to manage ringtones, track application performance, and protect against malware.

Each application category comes with the applications divided into the following categories, as shown in Figure 9-5:

- ✓ **Top Paid:** All apps in this category have a charge.

- ✓ **Top Free:** None of the apps in this category have a charge.

- ✓ **Just In:** These apps are relatively new, and might or might not have a charge.

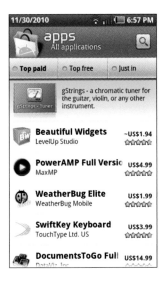

Figure 9-5: The Market Apps categories.

In general, you'll probably want to see what you get with a free application before you spend money on it. Many software companies know this, and offer a lower-feature version for free and an enhanced version for a charge. Enjoy the free-market mechanisms on this site and never feel regret for enjoying a free application.

What to Know Before You Buy

At least five organizations are involved when you buy an application:

- ✓ **Samsung:** Your phone manufacturer

- ✓ **Google:** Writers of the Android OS, and manager of the Android Market

- ✓ **Your cellular carrier:** Your wireless service provider

- ✔ **Visa, MasterCard, American Express, and Discover:** Payment vendors
- ✔ **The app developer:** The folks with the rights to apps that you download

All these folks want you to be happy with your phone and the apps that you buy. If things don't go well, though, you have a conundrum as to where to go for help.

In the days of the feature phone — that is, the phones that aren't smartphones — you could count on calling your cellular carrier. The phone manufacturer (in this case, Samsung) would have taught the customer service organization of your carrier on how to help you with issues.

However, it's not so simple with apps that you download from the Android Market or any other Internet storefront. Your carrier probably knows "something" about the apps that came with your phone, but you can't realistically expect your carrier to be the expert on all the hundreds of thousands of applications that you could download to your phone.

Avoiding Root applications

Some apps in the Android Market work only with phones with root access, also known as "rooted." Skip these apps. They're mostly not worth the hassle.

You can download most of the applications in the Android Market without problem. Some apps, however, work only on phones with root access. In my opinion, you're better off avoiding these applications.

The Android smartphone operating system is like the OS on your PC, but also has some protections to prevent applications from changing radio settings and other basic capabilities, intentionally or not, that could interfere with other cell phone users. You and I get little value getting to most of these advanced settings, but on occasion, some highly trained users may have a need to get past the standard security

to diagnose problems. These users have root access.

After you get past the standard security protections on your phone, some things no one should mess with. However, you can now do a few things with root access that were once prevented with standard security. For example, there are applications that you can acquire outside the Android market that allow you to turn your phone into a Wi-Fi access point for other Wi-Fi devices to connect through your phone. (The Sprint Epic 4G markets this as a feature, but the other phones don't allow it.)

Doing so would void the warranty on your phone and probably violate the terms of your service agreement, but it would work. And that's only if the rooting process worked. There is a possibility that trying to root your phone will cause it to lock up and stop working.

So, if you do run into difficulties with an app, be realistic about where to get support. Consider what you do now when you have a problem with a PC application. The Web site of the app developer is probably a good place to start. Toward the bottom of an application's description, apps in the Market provide you a Web site and/or e-mail for support. Haranguing the customer service representative from your carrier is probably not going to help.

Installing an Application on Your Phone

Downloading and installing an app on your Galaxy S phone is a snap. I'll walk you through downloading both free and paid apps, using WeatherBug as an example. For the purposes of this chapter, I assume that you've done some homework and decided to download a more sophisticated weather application than what comes with your phone. You've heard about the Android version of the WeatherBug, and you want to check it out.

1. **From the Home screen on your phone, tap the Android Market icon.**

   If the Android Market icon isn't on your Home screen, open your Applications list and find it there. This brings up the Android Market screen (refer to Figure 9-2).

2. **Tap the search button (the magnifying glass icon at the upper right of the screen; or, one of the Device Function keys at the bottom of the screen).**

   This brings up the search function within the Market. This screen is shown in Figure 9-6.

Figure 9-6: Search for apps in Android Market.

3. **From the keyboard that automatically pops up, type your search word(s) and then tap Enter.**

For this example, I entered **weatherbug**. The results are shown in Figure 9-7.

This search term results in four hits. Three versions are free, but note that the first hit, WeatherBug Elite, costs $1.99. (More on that in a bit.)

4. **Tap the application you want.**

For this example, go for the free version, regular ol' WeatherBug.

The description of the free WeatherBug application appears; see Figure 9-8.

The description page includes the app's title, its ratings summary and how many people have rated it, a description, comments, number of downloads, and its features. Of course, you'll see its price, as well as developer info. Too, from here, you can flag the app to Google as inappropriate should need be.

Figure 9-7: The search results for WeatherBug apps.

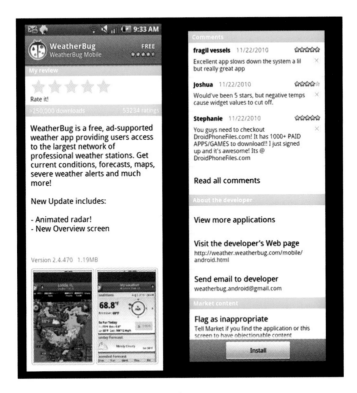

Figure 9-8: Read full descriptions of apps.

The number of downloads is a helpful nugget because you can get an idea whether you're a guinea pig, or this is a time-tested application. And don't overlook the developer information, where you can read about other applications the developer has written, a link to that developer's Web page, and a general e-mail contact address.

5. **If the app is free, proceed to the following section. If the app has a fee, go to the later section, "For fee."**

For free

You found an app you want, and it's free. Continuing with the steps in the preceding section, from the description page, do the following.

1. **Tap the Install button.**

   A warning screen appears with the functions that the application will have the ability to change. For example, if you proceed with the WeatherBug download, the app will have access to your location, and can access the Internet through your account, and can interact with some system tools on your phone.

2. **If you're good with the warning, tap OK to confirm that you want to proceed and to download the app.**

   The application download begins. First you get a pop-up alert that the process is starting. Then the notification area shows that the application is indeed downloading.

   If the download is interrupted because, say, your phone battery dies or you leave your coverage area, the download will pick up again where it left off as soon as you have a connection again. You don't have to do anything to make this happen.

   When the download process is over, a message appears on the notification screen, and the application icon will appear in your Applications list. (Read more about the notification screen in Chapter 2, and also later in the chapter where I discuss updates.)

You can now use the app. Go to the Application list, tap the application's icon, and have fun!

For fee

If the application you want to download isn't free, well, you have to pay for it. The Android Market doesn't take cash, money orders, checks, or anything in trade. It requires using Visa, MasterCard, American Express, or a Discover card.

So say that you're willing to pony up for the WeatherBug Elite app at $1.99.

1. **After you run your search for the app (refer to Figure 9-8), opt for the pay version by tapping WeatherBug Elite.**

   You get the same information-type of page (refer to Figure 9-8), but instead of an Install button, you see a Buy button, as shown in Figure 9-9.

2. **So, tap that Buy button.**

   A screen appears like the one in Figure 9-10. You need to have the following information handy:

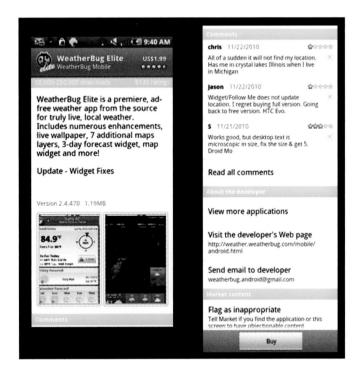

Figure 9-9: If it's a fee app, buy it here.

- Your name as it appears on your charge card
- The expiration date of the card
- The CVC (security) code on the back of the card
- Your billing address
- A telephone number

  It populates it with your cellular phone number, but you can over-write it with any number you want.

3. **Enter your information and tap Save.**

Google securely saves this information on your Gmail account for the future.

Figure 9-10: The credit card screen for Android Market checkout.

4. Tap OK to continue buying the app.

A pop-up message shows that Android Market is authorizing the purchase. Within a few seconds, you will get a chime on the notification area to indicate that your application is successfully installed. Done.

Getting Application Updates

Sometimes applications are updated by the developer, maybe to fix a bug or add new features. When this happens, assuming that you have that app, the manufacturer will let you know of the update by having Android Market send you a notification. This will appear on the Notification screen; read all about that in Chapter 2.

Even if you clear your notifications, you can still check whether any of your apps have an update and acquire those updates easily by looking through the Android Market and going to the list of all the apps that you've downloaded. Here's how:

1. **Open the Android Market application.**

2. **Tap the Menu button (of the Device Function keys).**

   This brings up the options within Market to search, look at the applications that you've downloaded, or get help. This screen is shown in Figure 9-11.

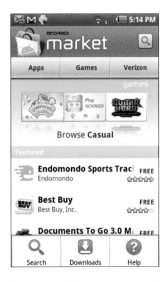

Figure 9-11: The menu pop-up from the Android Market home page.

3. **Tap the Downloads button.**

   As shown in Figure 9-12, all applications you've downloaded are listed. Also in the figure, you can see some updates that are available, including one for WeatherBug.

4. **Tap the application you wish to update.**

   This brings up a screen like that shown in Figure 9-13.

5. **If you're okay with the update, tap the Update button.**

   From this point, you follow the process of installing a new application.

Figure 9-12: View your downloaded apps to look for updates.

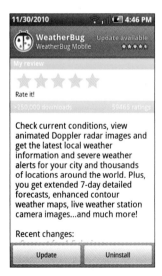

Figure 9-13: Read the update.

Why is Google checking my applications?

Knowing that Google is checking software on your phone might seem a little creepy or intrusive. However, most smartphones patrol preemptively in some form because malware can get control of a smartphone and make it violate laws or regulations from the Federal Communications Commission (FCC). Google — and all its competitors — tests mobile software for this; after all, malware can be either intentional (like a computer virus) or just careless programming.

So, focus on the benefits of Google's aggressive checking. First, there is much less of a chance that your phone will become unresponsive during an emergency, send your personal data to an identify thief, or give your location to a stalker. Plus, the system can automatically send bug fixes and upgrades to your software.

Getting Rid of an App

It happens. You download an app, sure that it would be the answer to all the time you spend on the bus or train or plane, only to find that the app isn't as cool as you thought it would be. Here's how to get rid of it:

1. **Open the Market application.**

2. **Tap the Menu button (of the Device Function keys).**

   This brings up the options for Market, as shown earlier in Figure 9-11.

3. **Tap Downloads button.**

   As shown in Figure 9-12, all applications you've purchased are listed.

4. **Press and hold the application you wish to uninstall.**

   This brings up a pop-up screen (see Figure 9-14), which offers you the options of

   • *Details:* The description screen of the application

   • *Open Application:* The same as if you just tapped the application to open it

   • *Uninstall:* That's the ticket!

Figure 9-14: Delete an app from here.

5. **Tap Uninstall.**

   You'll be prompted as to why you want the application to go away. Your choices are

   - I don't use or want it.
   - I need more space on my phone.
   - It's defective.
   - It's malicious.
   - I'd rather not say.

   These stock responses might cover your reason. Sadly, there is no way to say, "It was funny once or twice, but the application that makes it look as if my screen is broken got old fast."

6. **Choose whatever option you want and then tap OK.**

   The app is toast.

Part IV
Entertainment Applications

The 5th Wave   By Rich Tennant

"Okay, the view's just up ahead. Everyone open up the Camera app and get ready to be dazzled."

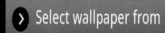

 Gallery

 Live wallpapers

 Wallpaper gallery

In this part . . .

ou can also use your Galaxy S phone for
strictly personal entertainment.

The Super AMOLED screen makes your phone
ideal for taking and viewing photos.

The bright screen and powerful processor on your
phone allow you to download and play immersive
games. Depending upon the title, you can play
nonstop or you can "snack" on your games as
your time allows.

The phone with its GPS receiver can take you
interesting places. You can also enjoy music,
video, and podcasts on your phone that you
download from your favorite storefront.

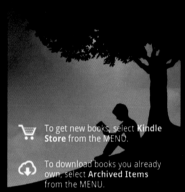

To get new books, select **Kindle Store** from the MENU.

To download books you already own, select **Archived Items** from the MENU.

| Wallpaper | Search |
| Edit page | Settings |

Sharing Pictures

In This Chapter

▶ Taking pictures and video on your phone

▶ Organizing your pictures and video

▶ Sharing pictures and video with friends and family

*1*f you're like many cellphone users, you love that you can shoot photographs and video with your phone. You probably carry your phone a lot more places than you carry your camera so you never again have to miss a great photograph because you left your camera at home.

And don't think that Samsung skimped on the camera on your Galaxy S. Boasting 5MP of muscle, this camera is complemented with lots of shooting options. Then, you can view your shots on that wicked Super AMOLED screen. Samsung also includes a Gallery app for organizing and sharing. Plus, the camera can shoot stills and video.

Stick with this chapter to see all this: how to take a photograph, organize your photos, and share them with friends and family.

A super-fast primer on Super AMOLED

All Samsung Galaxy S phones have a Super AMOLED screen. Allow me to take a moment to explain what makes this so good — and you so smart for having bought this technology within your Samsung Galaxy S phone.

To start, think about a typical LCD screen, like what you might use for your TV or PC. LCDs are great, but they work best indoors where it's not too bright. LCDs need a backlight (fluorescent, commonly), and the backlight draws a fair amount of power although much less power than a CRT. When used on a phone, an LCD screen is the largest single user of battery life, using more power than the radios or the processor. Also, because of the backlight on an LCD screen, when there was black on the screen, it wasn't a true black (kinda washed-out).

The next step has been to use light emitting diodes (LEDs), which convert energy to light more efficiently. Monochrome LEDs have been used for decades. They are also used in the mongo-screens in sports arenas. Until recently, getting the colors right (blue was a big problem) was a struggle. That problem was solved by using organic materials ("organic" as in carbon based, as opposed to no pesticides) for LEDs.

The first organic LEDs (OLEDs) looked good, drew less power, and offered really dark blacks — but still had two problems. They really stunk in bright light, even worse than LCD screens. Also there was a problem with "cross talk," where the individual pixels would get confused over time whether they were to be on or off.

The solution to the pixel's confusion is called Active Matrix, which tells the pixels more frequently whether they are to be on or off. When you have Active Matrix technology, you have an Active Matrix Organic LED, or AMOLED. This technology still stinks in bright light, however.

Enter the Super AMOLED technology, made by Samsung. When compared with the first AMOLED screens, Super AMOLED screens are 20 percent brighter, use 20 percent less power, and cut sunlight reflection by 80 percent. This is really super!

This screen still uses a significant share of battery life, but less than with earlier technologies. With Super AMOLED, you even save more power if you use darker backgrounds where possible.

Say Cheese! Taking a Picture with Your Phone

Before you can take a picture, you have to open the Camera app. The easiest way is to simply access the Camera application from the Application list. Just tap the Camera icon to launch the app.

With the Camera app open, you're ready to take a picture within a few seconds. The screen becomes your viewfinder. You'll see a screen like that shown in Figure 10-1.

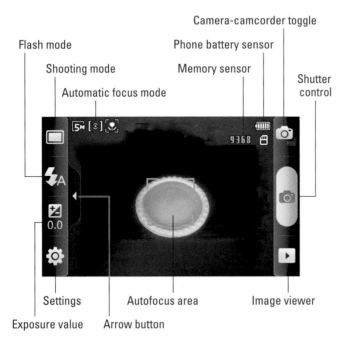

Figure 10-1: The screen is the viewfinder for the Camera app.

And how do you snap the picture? Just tap the big Camera icon on the right: the camera within the oval. The image that's in your viewfinder turns into a digital image that you can set to either JPG or PNG format. Easy as pie.

After you take a picture, you have a choice. The image is automatically stored in another application: Gallery. This allows you to keep on snapping away and come back to the Gallery when you have time. I cover the Gallery application more in the upcoming section, "Managing Your Photo Images."

However, if you want to send that image right away, here's what you do:

1. **From the viewfinder screen, tap the Forward icon.**

   This is the arrow pointing to the right at the bottom right of the screen. This brings up the screen shown in Figure 10-2.

2. **Tap the Share button on the lower-left portion of the screen.**

   This brings up the options you can use to forward the image; see Figure 10-3. These options include any of the following although your phone might not support all the options listed here. Only the options that are enabled will show up on your phone.

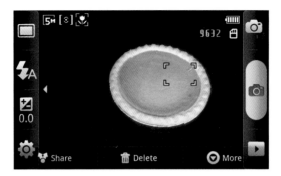

Figure 10-2: The image and your forwarding options.

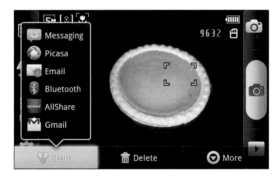

Figure 10-3: Forwarding options for the current image.

- *Messaging:* Attach the image to a text message to someone's phone as an MMS message.

- *Picasa:* Picasa is a Web site owned by Google, created to help its subscribers organize and share photos. The main advantage for subscribers is that they can send links to friends or family for them to see a thumbnail of images, rather than sending a large number of high resolution files. Read more on Picasa in the next section.

- *Email:* Send the image as an attachment with your primary e-mail account.

- *Bluetooth:* Send images to devices, such as a laptop or phone, linked with a Bluetooth connection.

- *AllShare:* This is an application that allows you to share with DLNA-compatible devices.

DLNA (Digital Living Network Alliance) is a trade group of several consumer electronics firms to create an in-home network among compatible devices. The goal is to make it easier to share music, videos, and photos. Your Galaxy S is DLNA compliant. If you have other DLNA devices, such as a TV, you can easily share your photos by using the AllShare app.

- *Gmail:* If your main e-mail is with Gmail, this option and the Email option are the same.

Of course, an account with Gmail (that is, an e-mail address that ends in @gmail.com) is entirely optional. However, there are advantages to having a Gmail account with your Android-based Galaxy S phone: For example, you automatically become a subscriber to Picasa and other Google-owned services.

When you select one of these options, the image will automatically be attached or uploaded, depending upon the nature of the service you selected. (I cover setting up your e-mail more in Chapter 6.)

For skeptics only

If you've ever used a cameraphone, you might be thinking, "Why make such a big deal about this camera's phone? Cameraphones aren't worth the megapixels they're made of." Granted, many cameraphones weren't quite as good as a digital camera, but Samsung has addressed these issues with the Galaxy S.

- **Resolution:** The resolution on most cameraphones is lower than what you typically get on a digital camera. The Galaxy S, though, sports a 5 megapixel (MP) camera — and that's good enough to produce a 4 x 6" print that's indistinguishable from what you could produce with a camera.

- **Photo transfer:** With most cameraphones, the photos are hard to move from the camera to a computer. With the Samsung Galaxy S, though (remember: It uses the Android operating system), you can quickly and easily send an image, or a bunch of images, anywhere you want, easily and wirelessly.

- **Screen resolution:** In practice, many cameraphone users just end up showing their pictures to friends right on their phones. Many cameraphone screens, however, don't have very good resolution, which means your images don't look so hot when you want to show them off to your friends. The good news is the Samsung Galaxy S has a bright, high-resolution screen. Photos look really good on the Super AMOLED–technology screen.

- **Organization:** Most cameraphones don't offer much in the way of organization tools. Your images are all just there on your phone, without any structure. But the Samsung Galaxy S has the Gallery application that makes organizations of your photos easier. It is also set up to share these photos with a great deal of ease.

Getting a Little Fancier with Your Camera

Using the default Camera settings to snap pics is perfectly fine for those candid, casual, on-the-go shots: say, friends in your well-lit living room. However, your Samsung Galaxy S phone camera can support much more sophisticated shots. I cover the main options here, but if you want to get a lot fancier, play around with the settings to your heart's content.

The Mode setting

The Mode setting is where you make some basic settings that describe the situation under which you will be taking your shot. The default is a single picture. The Mode icon is shown in Figure 10-4 and is visible in Figure 10-1 and 10-2 on the upper-left corner of the viewfinder.

You actually don't see the icons along the left part of the viewfinder until you tap the arrow button — then, the icons scroll onto the viewfinder. Otherwise, they're tucked away.

Figure 10-4: The Mode icons on the camera viewfinder.

Tapping the Mode icon brings up a number of choices:

- ✔ **Single Shot:** Taking a single photo at a time is the default setting.
- ✔ **Beauty:** This mode automatically hides subtle facial imperfections. (No guarantees!)
- ✔ **Smile Shot:** In this setting, the camera "looks" at the people in the viewfinder and automatically takes the shot when it detects a smile.

✔ **Continuous:** This setting takes a quick series of six images per second for each press on the Camera icon; that way, you can later pick which one you really want. This option uses the same amount of memory and battery as taking six shots, which isn't much. And it makes it more likely that everyone's eyes will be open!

✔ **Panorama:** Take a wider shot than you can with a single shot. Press the Camera button while you rotate through your desired field of view. The application then digitally stitches the individual photos into a single, wide angle shot.

✔ **Vintage:** This option magically makes your new photo look like an older photo, such as making everything look like a daguerreotype.

✔ **Add Me:** You use this option when you're taking a group photo, and there is no friendly stranger to take the shot. You select this option and snap the picture of the group but minus yourself. Then everyone in the group freezes, except for one volunteer. The volunteer gets the camera, you hop into the shot, and the volunteer takes the picture of you and everyone else. The application then merges the two images together to make it look like everyone is in one shot at the same time!

✔ **Action Shot:** This setting shortens the duration of the shot to help eliminate blur.

✔ **Cartoon:** The cartoon setting takes your image and converts it into a high contrast image that looks like a cartoon. A sample is shown in Figure 10-5.

Figure 10-5: Shooting with the Cartoon option.

Don't use the Cartoon setting for your annual holiday card, or you'll never hear the end of it from your mother-in-law.

More complicated image editing might be easier on your desktop computer. However, you can make some edits on your phone and send them off right away. Your choice.

Pick which option sounds right and snap away.

Settings

If the Galaxy S shooting modes (listed in the previous section) aren't enough, you can find about a dozen more options under the Scene settings. If these don't show on your viewfinder, you can find them by going into the Settings. There, you can find other options like Night mode, Dawn mode, Sunset, Fireworks, and Candlelight. This is accessed by tapping the cog icon on the viewfinder. Many of the scene options are shown in Figure 10-6.

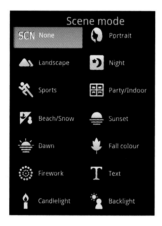

Figure 10-6: Scene mode options.

In addition, you can set more than a dozen options to adjust contrast, image quality, and other advanced stuff. The settings include the options shown in Figure 10-7.

Flash

If your phone is a Verizon Fascinate or a Sprint Epic 4G, your camera has a built-in flash. This feature won't light up the Grand Canyon from the window seat on your airplane, but it's better than nothing.

The AT&T Captivate and T-Mobile Vibrant do not have a flash.

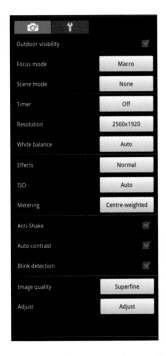

Figure 10-7: Camera settings options.

To change the auto-flash default setting — the camera will flash if the camera thinks it needs some more brightness — tap the lightning bolt icon. Sometimes, for example, you don't want the flash, even if the camera thinks that you do. Other times, you want a flash, even when it's otherwise bright.

Digital magnification

If you want to control how much background you see in your shot, Samsung has a slick way to zoom in on a shot. When you're in Camera mode, you can use the volume buttons to zoom in and out.

- **Reduce volume:** Press this button to zoom in.

- **Increase volume:** Press this button to zoom out.

You might find the digital magnification capability by accident. When you hold the phone horizontally to use as a viewfinder, the buttons are on the bottom. This is often where you hold the phone.

The Digital Camcorder in Your Pocket

Your Samsung Galaxy S Camera application can also function as a digital camcorder. All you need to do is to put your camera into Camcorder mode. Then, recording video is simply a matter of pressing the Record button; see this icon in Figure 10-8, with a red dot in an oval to the right side of the viewfinder.

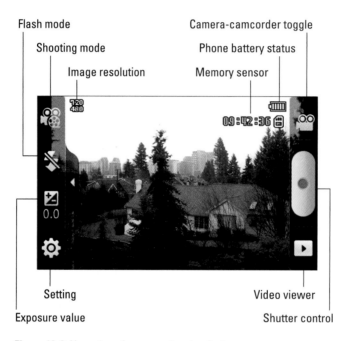

Figure 10-8: Your phone's camcorder viewfinder.

Your phone is not only recording the video, but it's also recording the sound. Be careful what you say!

Starting the camcorder

The only challenge with using the camcorder is finding the correct button that switches the phone from still Camera mode to Camcorder mode. For this, you need to determine which version of the Galaxy S you have.

Verizon Fascinate and Sprint Epic

If you look back at Figure 10-1, you see two camera icons on the right part of the screen. The camera icon (it's a dark camera) in the big oval is for snapping a still picture. Right above that icon is another camera icon, not in an oval; note that this camera icon is light. These are shown in Figure 10-9.

Figure 10-9: The Switch to Camcorder Mode
icon (left) and Take Picture icon (right).

The light, upper camera icon tells you that you are in Camera mode. This
isn't intuitively obvious why two similar icons would have different meanings, but if this is the worst case of confusing icons, you're in good shape.

To move to the camcorder, you leave Camera mode by tapping the light (that
is, the upper) camera icon. A silhouette of a light camcorder appears. You
are now in Camcorder mode. To toggle back to still camera mode, tap the
camcorder icon. This will return the light camera silhouette.

AT&T Captivate

The Captivate solves this little problem by offering an icon with a light camera
pointing to a grayed out camcorder icon. To switch back to still camera mode,
there is a light camcorder icon with an arrow pointing to a camera icon. That
makes a little more sense.

T-Mobile Vibrant

The Vibrant takes a different tack on this altogether. When you're in the viewfinder mode for the still camera and you tap the arrow that opens the icons,
the Vibrant shows the camcorder silhouette on the upper-left of the screen.

The inference is that you can figure out that you're in still Camera mode, but
that if you want to switch to Camcorder mode, tap the camcorder icon. When
in Camcorder mode, tap the camera to move back to Camera mode.

Taking and sharing videos with your camcorder

If you started recording a video by tapping the oval with the red dot in the
viewfinder, perhaps knowing how to stop recording would be good. When
you're filming, a pause button and a stop button appear in the viewfinder

where the red-dot-oval was. You tap these buttons, shown in Figure 10-10, to pause or stop.

Figure 10-10: The Pause and Stop buttons in the camcorder viewfinder.

Just as you share photos you take with the camera, you can immediately share a video you recorded, play it, or delete it by tapping the video viewer. Also, the video is immediately saved on your camera. It is stored in the Gallery app (described later in this chapter) or is viewable from your Video Player app (covered in Chapter 13). Unlike the Gallery app for photos (described in the next section), you need to send a video as an attachment to either an e-mail or a text message.

You can get fancy with some of the settings for your camcorder, but you won't find nearly as many settings as you have for your camera (fortunately!). You can access the different options (shown in Figure 10-11) by tapping the Settings icon.

Figure 10-11: The Camcorder setting options.

Under most circumstances, you get the best results by leaving the default settings as they are — unless you want to save memory space by reducing your resolution or get really creative by using black-and-white mode effects.

Managing Your Photo Images

After you take some great pictures, you need to figure out what to do with them. Earlier in this chapter, I describe how to send an image immediately to another site. This will likely be the exception, though.

In most cases, it's easier to keep on doing what you were doing and go back to the Gallery application when you have some time to take a look at the images and then decide what to do with them. Your choices include the following:

- Store them on your phone within the Gallery app.
- Transfer them to your PC to your photo album application by sending them with e-mail.
- Store them on an Internet site, like Picasa or Flickr.
- Print them from your PC.
- Any combination of the above.

This chapter covers how to do each of these options.

Unlike many regular cellphones with a built-in camera, the Galaxy S makes it easier to access these choices. You need to determine the approach or approaches you want to take to keep your images when you want them. The rest of this chapter goes through your options.

Even though the Camera application and the Gallery application are closely related, they are two separate apps. Be sure that you keep straight which application you want to use.

The icon to launch the Gallery application is shown in Figure 10-12.

Figure 10-12: The Gallery icon.

The Gallery home page (shown in Figure 10-13) shows how the app first sorts the images on your phone into folders, depending upon where they originated.

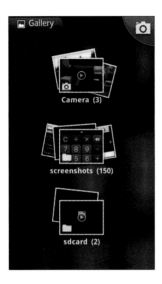

Figure 10-13: The home page for the Gallery app.

All your photos from the Camera app are placed in a folder called Camera. The videos that you take are placed in a folder called Videos. Otherwise, the folders will include any apps that use images, as shown in Figure 10-13.

To see an image, tap the appropriate folder. Within a folder, photos are displayed chronologically. An open folder is shown in Figure 10-14.

The default setting is to hide the date and time stamp. Showing the date and time stamp is simple, though, if that's your preference. In the upper-right corner of the folder is a toggle. When the switch is to the left, the 3 x 4 grid of dots is selected and the photos display without a time stamp.

When you tap the toggle, it moves to the right to select what looks like two pages. This setting shows photos sorted by time; see Figure 10-15. The folder groups the images taken on a given day.

Figure 10-14: An open folder within the Gallery app.

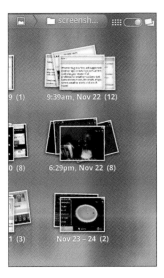

Figure 10-15: A Gallery folder with the time stamp on.

Using Images on Your Phone

In addition to sharing photos from your camera, your Galaxy S phone allows you to use a Gallery photo as wallpaper or as a photo for a contact. And if the fancy shooting settings in the Camera application aren't enough, you can wrangle minor edits — as in, crop or rotate — when you have an image in the Gallery application.

The first step is to find the image that you want in Gallery. Typically, you'll find your image in your Camera folder among the most recent images. Tap the image that you want. This brings up a screen like that shown in Figure 10-16.

Figure 10-16: Open the image from
Gallery that you want to edit.

Tap the Menu hyperlink; then tap the More hyperlink. This brings up a menu of options, as shown in Figure 10-17.

  ✔ **Details:** See the information on the image: its metadata, which is fixed and cannot change.

  ✔ **Set As:** Make this image your wallpaper or set it as the image for a contact. (Read more on this in Chapter 5.)

✔ **Crop:** Cut away unnecessary or distracting parts of the image. The application creates a virtual box around what it considers to be the main object. You can move the box around the image, but you cannot resize it. You then can either save this cropped image or discard.

✔ **Rotate Left or Rotate Right:** The last two options allow you to rotate the image right or left. This is useful if you turned the camera sideways to get more height in your shot and now want to turn the image to landscape (or vice versa).

Figure 10-17: Choose from options in Gallery.

Deleting an image

Not all the images on your phone are keepers. This is particularly true if you're using the Continuous option to take a quick series of images. (Read about Continuous shooting earlier in this chapter.)

When you want to get rid of an image, press and hold the image you want to delete. In a second, a green check box appears on that image, and a Delete icon appears at the bottom of the screen next to a trash can icon.

If you want to delete this image, tap Delete. The camera will verify that this is your intent. After you confirm, the image goes away.

Note that grayed-out check boxes appear on all the other images in the folder.

To delete more than one image, tap the gray icon. It will turn green, and then you tap Delete. Poof! They're gone forever. As shown in Figure 10-18, I tapped two images to prepare them for deletion. You can delete as many photos at one time as you are willing to tap.

When I say that the photos you delete are gone forever, I do mean *for-ev-er.* Most of us have inadvertently deleted the only copy of an image from a PC or a digital camera. That's not a pleasant feeling, so be careful.

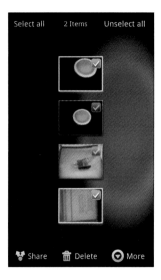

Figure 10-18: Deleting options.

In this app, the green checkmark means that you *do* want to delete it. The gray check mark means that you *do not* want to delete it. Getting these two options reversed leads to undesired results. See the previous Warning icon.

Viewing images on your phone

The Super AMOLED screen on your Galaxy S is a great way to enjoy your photos and share them with family and friends. Depending upon the circumstances, you can view images one at a time or as a slideshow.

To see one image at a time, just tap that image. See a series of images by tap-ping Slideshow, which brings up the next image in chronological order, every four seconds. The Slideshow icon is at the bottom of the image you're view-ing (refer to Figure 10-16).

Choosing a picture as wallpaper

To use a picture from your Gallery as wallpaper, follow these steps from your home page:

1. **Tap the Menu button.**

   This brings up a pop-up at the bottom of the screen.

2. **Tap the Wallpaper icon.**

   The screen shown in Figure 10-19 appears.

Figure 10-19: The Wallpaper options pop-up screen.

3. **Tap the Gallery icon.**

   This opens your photo Gallery.

4. **Tap the picture you want and then tap Save.**

   The image is immediately put onto the background of your home page.

To use a static background instead of one of your photos, tap Wallpaper Gallery (the bottom option of Figure 10-19). For Step 4, tap the background that you want and then tap Save.

The Live Wallpapers option of Figure 10-19 is more interesting. This kind of wallpaper moves around by itself and reacts subtly to touch. You might find this fascinating or distracting. No problem. Changing your background is simple.

If you like Live Wallpapers but don't like the options on your phone, you can access more options at the Android Market. Some are free, and others are for a fee.

Sharing Your Photos

Organizing your photos into albums is important. After you've been taking photos for a while, the job of organizing gets more difficult. You can't remember whether that picture of Johnny was from spring break or Easter. Start putting your pictures in albums sooner rather than later!

You can try to do this in the Gallery, but unfortunately, Gallery isn't really set up to handle your entire photo library.

There are a number of options that you have to get the photos off your phone so you can sort, edit, and organize them. I discuss how to do this with a single image at the beginning of the chapter. It's straightforward to do this with multiple images from within a given folder from the Gallery application.

Select the photos you want to share by pressing and holding on an image. Then tap the Share icon, which is also visible at the bottom of the screen in Figure 10-18.

When you tap Share, the pop-up for the Share options appears (see Figure 10-20). From this pop-up, you select your sharing option. The multiple images are all handled in one group. ***Note:*** This is the same list of sharing options you have for a single photo or video.

As I mention earlier, there is much to be said about storing your digital images on the Internet at an image hosting site like Picasa. If you have a Gmail account, you already have a Picasa account. If not, just register with Picasa at `http://picasa.google.com`.

Picasa isn't the only image-hosting site on the block. Flickr and Windows Live Photo Gallery are also available, to name a few. The advantage of using Picasa is that because the Android operating system and Picasa are both owned by Google, Picasa is already integrated into the system. It's not heroic to use the other sites, but that discussion goes beyond the scope of this book.

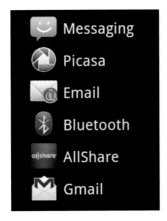

Figure 10-20: Bulk-sharing options from Gallery.

The advantages of using Picasa include

- **The storage capacity is huge.** You might have a large memory card in your phone, but the storage available on any image hosting site will dwarf what you have.

  When you upload to Picasa, a copy of the images remains on your phone. You might want to keep it there, or you might want to delete it after you transferred the images successfully to make more room on your phone.

  When you transfer a bunch of photos, their check boxes remain either checked or unchecked after they're sent. You can immediately delete what you just transferred without having to recheck every image.

- **It's professionally backed up.** How many of us have lost photos? How many of us have lost phones? 'Nuff said.

- **Picasa is free.** Google offers this service at no charge.

- **Access your images wherever you have Internet access.** Although showing pictures on your phone is great, Gallery isn't set up to host your complete photo library. Picasa can.

- **Others can see your images with links.** Rather than sending the full 5MB image of your kids for each of the 25 images of a birthday party, just send the link. Granny might want all the shots in high resolution, which she can do. Your college roommate probably is fine with the low resolution images on the Picasa site. No need to clog your old pal's inbox (unless you want to).

✔ **You control who has access.** Picasa allows you to set up access to selected groups. You can set it so that family has more access than your co-workers, for example.

✔ **You can order prints of images from your PC.** Picasa allows you to order prints from your PC without the need to transfer the images to another storage medium for you to then trudge down to a store to get prints.

✔ **There are tools to help you sort your images.** Gallery has limited control over your folders. Picasa, in contrast, can get very granular on how you set up your image folder hierarchy. You can get fancy, or you can keep it very simple. Your choice.

Saving to Picasa is easier than sending an e-mail if you have a Gmail account. Tap the Picasa sharing option, and it will upload that image; see Figure 10-21.

Figure 10-21: The information for Picasa to share a photo from Gallery.

After you verify the information, tap the Upload button, and off it goes to your Picasa site. This is shown in Figure 10-22.

When you access this site from your PC, it will ask you to register. After you do, you can see all your images sent from your phone. Figure 10-23 shows my picture on the Web.

I can now create a folder to store the image, edit the image, or share it on other Web services. All this is as easy as pie!

Figure 10-22: A Picasa upload in process.

Figure 10-23: My drop box on Picasa.

Playing Games

In This Chapter

▸ Perusing the games available on Android Market

▸ Downloading games to your phone

▸ Leaving feedback for games

▸ Keeping track of what you've downloaded

Games are the most popular kind of download for smartphones of all kinds. In spite of the focus on business productivity, socializing, and making your life simpler, games outpace all other application downloads. The electronic gaming industry has larger revenues than the movie industry — and has for several years!

The fact of the matter is that your Samsung Galaxy S, with its large Super AMOLED screen, makes Android-based games more fun. And seeing as how you already have a Galaxy, time to take a break and concentrate on having fun! Your phone will come with a few games preloaded on it. You can get a taste of what you can enjoy if you look for these in your Application list.

And when you're ready to look for more, this chapter shows you how to download new games from Android Market.

Using games doesn't drain the battery any more than using a normal application. However, really good games are immersive, which might cause you to lose track of time and potentially use up your battery if you're having too much fun.

Exploiting the Android Market Games Category

The Games category of Android Market is huge, and it includes everything from simple puzzles to simulated violence. All games involve various combinations of intellect, skill (either competitive or motor), and role playing.

You can access the games that I write about on Android Market. As discussed in Chapter 9, you bring up this application by tapping the Android Market icon (see Figure 11-1) on your Home screen or your App list.

Figure 11-1: The Android Market Icon.

Games are divided in Android Market (as shown in Figure 11-2) and fall into the following genres:

Figure 11-2: The Android Market Games home page.

> ✔ **Arcade & Action**
>
> - *Racing and flying:* Cars, go-karts, snowboards, jet skis, biplanes, jets, or spacecraft competing with one another

- *Shooting:* Projectiles from bullets to marshmallows to anti-ballistic missiles

- *Sports and recreation:* Electronic interpretations of real-world activities that incorporate some of the skill or strategy elements of the original game; vary based upon the level of detail

- *Fighting:* Fighting (combat) games; vary based upon the level of gore

- *Arcade:* Game room and bar favorites

✔ **Brain & Puzzle**

- *Educational:* Enjoyable while offering users enhanced skills or information

- *Puzzles and trivia:* Includes games like Sudoku, word search, and Trivial Pursuit

- *Strategy and simulation:* Emphasize decision-making skills, like chess; a variety of games with varying levels of complexity and agreement with reality

✔ **Cards & Casino**

- *Card and board games:* Versions of familiar (and some not so familiar) board and card games

- *Casino games:* Simulations of gambling games; no real money

✔ **Casual**

- Games that you can easily pick up and put aside

Some games might appear in more than one genre.

Looking at a game genre

Figure 11-3 shows the screen you see when you tap the Cards & Casino games genre.

Under the Cards & Casino title, you see three categories that are comparable to what I cover in Chapter 9 for other apps:

✔ **Top Paid:** These games will cost you money. A typical game costs from $0.99 to about $2.99. A more complicated game ranges in price from $2.99 to as much as $5.99. Only a few games cost more than $6.

✔ **Top Free:** These games don't cost you money. Go figure.

✔ **Just In:** Free or for a fee, these games are new.

Figure 11-3: The Android Market
Cards & Casino games page.

You can tap any of these to get ideas for games you might want to acquire.
Or, if you already know what you want, go fish. To find a specific game,
simply enter the name of the game in the search box that comes up when you
tap the magnifying glass at the top of the screen or press the Search key of
the Device Function keys after you enter Android Market.

Knowing what to look for in a genre

When you're not sure of what game to buy and you're in a genre that looks
promising, look for these road signs to help you check out and narrow your
choices among similar titles:

- **Ratings/comments:** Gamers love to exalt good games and bash bad ones.
- **Just In:** Check out recently released games that replace a previous
  release that proved successful.
- **Developer:** If you have a positive experience with a given developer,
  you can reasonably expect that other titles from this organization would
  offer another positive experience.
- **Internet research:** Some poking around on the Internet will tell you
  about games that are popular with others that share your preferences.

✏ **Price:** As a tie breaker among similar titles, a slightly higher price is a final indication of a superior game. And because you're talking only a few pennies, price isn't usually a big deal.

These road signs are either categories within a description or are categories used for sorting within a genre.

Examining a particular game

When you find a game that you want to acquire, you can access its description and find out a bit more. Figure 11-4 shows a panorama of a game description.

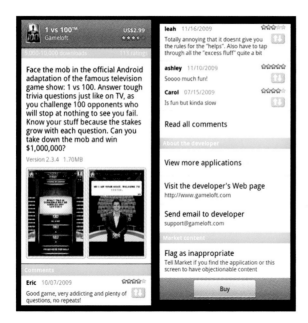

Figure 11-4: A game description.

The description gives an overview of the game from the company as well as feedback left by the game's users. After you download a game, you can leave feedback, and I tell you how later in this chapter.

At the bottom of this description is a Buy button: After all, this game comes for a fee. Tapping Buy takes you through the payment process I present in Chapter 9. Free games have an Install button.

Other places to get Android apps

It's time to come clean. You can indeed get Android games and apps from places other than the Android Market. The larger storefronts include PocketGear, GetJar, MobileRated, Handmark, Handango, and MobiHand. These storefronts are a good alternative if you're seeking games and apps that are out of the mainstream. And some storefronts also specialize in apps or games that are strictly for mature audiences.

As a rule, you need to register with a screen name and a good password. A good password is important because you might also want to leave your credit card number on the site to pay for your purchases, just like at Android Market.

The process for downloading apps is similar although not identical to downloading from Market. One difference with most of these sites is that you need to identify the phone you plan to use with the app. This way, those vendors present only the apps that work on your phone.

Downloading a game

Here's how to download a game:

1. **Tap the Install or Buy button.**

   If the game is free, it's Install. If there is a fee, it's Buy. In either case, a warning screen appears to show you the functions of your phone that the application will have the ability to change.

2. **If you're good with the warning, tap OK to confirm that you want to proceed and to download the app.**

   The application download begins. First you get a pop-up alert that the process is starting. Then the notification screen shows that the application is indeed downloading.

Getting game updates

Sometimes games are updated by the developer. When this happens, Android Market will send you a notification that appears in the Notification screen (discussed in Chapter 2). In case you're interested in acquiring the update, the following steps take you through the process:

1. **Open the Android Market application.**

2. **Tap the Menu button (of the Device Function keys).**

   This brings up options (at the bottom of the screen) to search the market, look at the applications you've downloaded, or get help. Figure 11-5 shows these options.

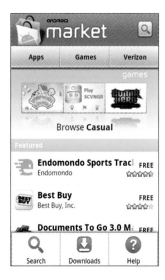

Figure 11-5: Menu pop-up from the Market home page.

3. **Tap the Downloads button.**

   You see a screen (similar to Figure 11-6) that lists all the games and applications you've purchased.

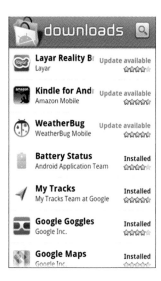

Figure 11-6: Games and apps you've downloaded from Android Market.

4. **Tap the application you wish to update.**

This brings up the screen shown in Figure 11-7.

Games include Chuck Norris jokes. Did you know that Chuck Norris can divide by zero?

Figure 11-7: Information screen for an app with an available update.

5. **Tap Update.**

From this point, just follow the process of installing a new application.

Some games and apps offer the option to automatically update. If you check Allow Automatic Updating, the app or game can update itself without you needing to take any action. It is convenient, but only allow this with reliable publishers!

Leaving Feedback on Games

Android Market for applications (in general) and games (in particular) is a very free market. When you come in to the Market, your best path to finding what would make for a good purchase is to read the reviews of those that have gone before you.

After you're experienced, you can help make the system work by providing your own review of a game that you have downloaded and used. This section gives you the process.

Start at the first screen of Android Market by tapping the icon on the Home screen or App list.

1. **Tap the Menu icon.**

   This brings up a pop-up like the image shown in Figure 11-8.

Figure 11-8: The Menu pop-up for the Android Market applications.

2. **Tap the Downloads icon.**

   This brings up the applications that you've downloaded, as shown in Figure 11-9.

3. **Tap the game for which you'd like to leave feedback.**

   Tapping the title of the game normally brings up the game description, like that shown in Figure 11-4. After you've downloaded a game, though, the screen changes to give you the opportunity to leave feedback, as shown in Figure 11-10.

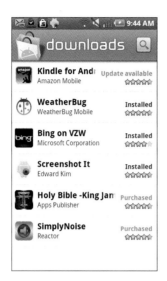

Figure 11-9: Check out your downloads.

Figure 11-10: The game description page with space for feedback.

4. **Tap the stars on the screen.**

   This brings up a pop-up screen, as shown on the left of Figure 11-11.

Figure 11-11: The ratings stars pop-up screen before and after entering feedback.

5. **Tap the number of stars that you believe this game deserves. When you're done, tap OK.**

   The right image of Figure 11-11 shows the result for a four-star review.

   At this point, you can enter any comments. You cannot enter comments without first choosing the number of stars for this game, though. The result looks like Figure 11-12.

Figure 11-12: The game description page with space for comments.

6. **Carefully enter your comments in the pop-up screen area.**

   When you tap the text box for comments, the pop-up screen shown in Figure 11-13 appears.

Figure 11-13: The game description page with space for comments.

7. **When you're done entering your feedback, tap the OK button.**

   Your comments are sent to Android Market for everyone to see. For the sake of the system, make sure that your comments are accurate!

Uninstalling a Game

Say that you played a game, and you doubt that you want to play it again. Here's how to get rid of a game from the Download list:

1. **Open the Market application.**

2. **Tap the Menu button of the Device Function keys.**

3. **Tap the Downloads button.**

4. **Press and hold on the application that you want to uninstall.**

   This brings up a screen that offers you an uninstall option (refer to Figure 11-7).

5. **Tap the Uninstall button.**

   You're prompted to tell why you want the application to go away. Your choices are

   - I don't use or want it.

   - I need more space on my phone.

   - It's defective.

   - It's malicious.

   - I'd rather not say.

6. **Choose the option that describes your reason for uninstalling and then tap OK.**

   It's gone.

Mapping Out Where You Want to Be

In This Chapter

▶ Deciding what you want to use for navigation

▶ Using what's already on your phone

▶ Using maps safely

*H*aving a map on your phone is a very handy tool. At the most basic level, you can ask your phone to show you a map for where you plan to go. This is convenient, but only a small part of what you can do.

With the right applications, your Galaxy S phone can do all the following:

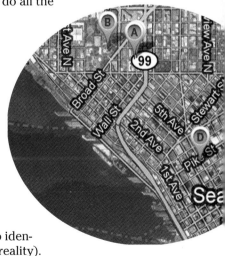

✔ Automatically find your location on a map.

✔ Give directions to where you want to go:

- As you drive, using historical driving times

- As you drive, using real-time road conditions

- While you walk

- As you take public transportation

✔ Give turn-by-turn directions as you travel.

✔ Tell others where you are.

✔ Use the screen on your phone as a viewfinder to iden-tify landmarks as you pan the area (augmented reality).

There are also some mapping applications for commercial users, such as CoPilot Live Truck from ALK Technologies, but I don't cover them in this chapter.

GPS 101: First Things First

You can't talk having smartphone mapping without GPS in the background, which creates a few inherent challenges about which you need to be aware. First off (and obviously), there is a GPS receiver in your phone. That means the following:

- **Gimme a sec.** Like all GPS receivers, your location-detection system takes a little time to determine your location when you first turn on your phone.

- **Outdoors is better.** Many common places where you use your phone — primarily, within buildings — have poor GPS coverage.

- **Nothing is perfect.** Even with good GPS coverage, location and mapping aren't perfected yet. *Augmented reality,* the option that identifies local landmarks on the screen, is even less perfect.

- **Turn me on.** Your GPS receiver must be turned on for it to work. Sure, turning it off saves battery life but precludes it from working for mapping applications.

- **Keep it on the down-low.** Sharing your location information is of grave concern to privacy advocates. The fear is that a stalker or other villain can access your location information in your phone to track your movements. In practice, there are easier ways to accomplish this goal, but controlling who knows your location is still something you should consider, particularly when you have applications that share your location information. See the section, "Letting Others Know Where You Are," later in this chapter.

Good cellular coverage has nothing to do with GPS coverage. The GPS receiver in your phone is looking for satellites; cellular coverage is based upon antennas mounted on towers or tall buildings.

Mapping apps are useful, but they also use more battery life and data than many other applications. Be aware of the impact on your data usage and battery life. It is convenient to leave mapping applications active.

Practically Speaking: Using Maps

The kind of mapping application that's easiest to understand is one that you open the application, and it presents a local map. Depending upon the model of your phone, you will have mapping applications preloaded, such as Google Maps, TeleNav, or VZ Navigator. These are found both on your Home screen and in your Application list.

It's not a large leap for a smartphone to offer directions from your GPS-derived location to somewhere you want to go in the local area. These are standard capabilities found in each of these applications.

This section describes Google Maps and Google Maps Navigation; these are both free and might come preinstalled on your phone. Other mapping applications that might come with your phone, such as Bing Maps or TeleNav, have similar capabilities, but the details will be a bit different. Or, you might wish to use other mapping applications. That's all fine.

As a rule, free navigation applications, like Google Maps Navigation, use historical averages for travel times. The applications that charge a modest monthly fee (between $5 and $10 monthly), like VZ Navigator, have real-time updates that avoid taking you on congested routes. So if you depend on your mapping app to get where you're going on a regular basis, you might find it worth your while to spend money for a paid app.

In addition to the general-purpose mapping applications that come on your phone, hundreds of mapping applications are available that can help you find a favorite store, navigate waterways, or find your car in a crowded parking lot. For example, Navigon and TCS offer solutions that base navigation on real-time traffic conditions. The Parking Lot Android app can help you find your car in a large parking lot.

As nice as mapping devices are, they're too slow to tell you to stop looking at them and avoid an oncoming car. If you can't control yourself in the car and need to watch the arrow on the map screen move, do yourself a favor and let someone else drive. If no one else is available to drive, be safe and don't use the navigation service on your phone in the car.

The most basic way to use a map is to bring up the Google Maps application. The icon for launching this app is shown in Figure 12-1.

Figure 12-1: The Maps icon.

The first screen that you see when you tap the Maps icon is a street map with your location. Figure 12-2 shows an example of a map when the phone user is in Seattle.

Center map on your location

Layers

Nearby services

Zoom in or out

Location of friends (if enabled)

Figure 12-2: You start where you are.

The location of the user is at the center of the map. The resolution of the map in the figure starts at about one square mile. You can see other parts of the map by placing a finger on the map and dragging away from the part of the map that you want to see. That brings new sections of the map onto the screen.

Turn the phone to change how the map is displayed. Depending on what you're looking for, a different orientation might be easier.

Changing map scale

A resolution of one square mile will work under some circumstances to help you get oriented in an unfamiliar place. But sometimes it helps to zoom out to get a broader perspective, or zoom in to help you find familiar landmarks, like a body of water or a major highway.

To get more real estate onto the screen, use the pinch motion as discussed in Chapter 2. This shrinks the size of the map and brings in more of the map around where you're pinching. If you need more real estate on the screen, you can keep pinching until you get more and more map. After you have your bearings, you can return to the original resolution by double-tapping the screen.

On the other hand, a scale of one square mile might not be enough. To see more landmarks, use the stretch motion to zoom in. The stretch motion expands the boundaries of the place where you start the screen. Continue stretching and stretching until you get to the detail that you want. Figure 12-3 shows a street map both zoomed in and zoomed out.

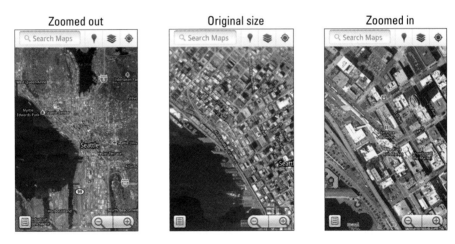

Figure 12-3: A street image zoomed in and zoomed out.

You can also tap the plus sign on the lower right-hand corner to zoom in and the minus sign to zoom out.

If you're zooming in and can't find where you are on the map, tap the dot-surrounded-by-a-circle icon (refer to Figure 12-2). It moves the map so that you're in the center.

Finding nearby services

Most searches for services fall into a relatively few categories. Your Maps application is set up to find what you're most likely to seek. By tapping the Services icon (refer to Figure 12-2) you're offered a quick way to find the services near you, such as restaurants, coffee shops, bars, hotels, attractions, ATMs, and gas stations, as shown in Figure 12-4.

Figure 12-4: Tap to find a service on the map.

Just tap one of the topical icons, and your phone will perform a search of businesses in your immediate area. The results come back as a regular Google search with its name, address, and distance from your location.

Then tap one of the options to see more details on that business; see the result in Figure 12-5.

In addition to the location and reviews are four icons:

✔ A map of where you are in relation to this business

✔ A Right Turn sign that offers you turn-by-turn directions from where you are to this business

You might need to download Google Maps Navigation to your phone to get the turn-by-turn directions. This is a free app from the Android Market. To download this, turn to Chapter 9.

Figure 12-5: The detailed results of a service selection.

🖛 A phone icon, which you can tap to call the business

🖛 More options, which include

 • *Street View:* See the location in Google Street View. As shown in Figure 12-6, Street View shows a photo of the street address for the location you entered.

 • *Share This Place:* Send a contact (or contacts) information about this location, via e-mail or text message.

 • *Search Nearby:* Look around in case you're not totally satisfied with this selection.

 • *Buzz about This Place:* Read more than just what's in the reviews.

 • *Add as a Contact:* Add this business to your contacts.

 • *Report a Problem:* Let Google know if something is wrong with its information, such as if the place isn't there, or there is incorrect information about this location.

 • *More Info:* Run another Google search on this business to get additional information, such as reviews from other parts of the Web.

Just how deeply you dive into using this information is up to you. In any case, having this kind of information when you're visiting an unfamiliar location is handy.

Figure 12-6: A Street View shot of a location.

Getting and Using Directions

You probably want to get directions from your map application. I know I do. You can get directions in a number of ways, including

- ✔ Tap the Search text box and enter the name or address of your location: for example, "Seattle Space Needle" or "742 Evergreen Terrace, Springfield, IL."

- ✔ Tap the Search icon of the Device Function keys and enter your location.

- ✔ Tap the Services icon (refer to Figure 12-2), tap the Attractions icon (refer to Figure 12-4), and select your location.

Any of these methods lead you to the map showing your location, as shown in Figure 12-7.

It might seem intuitive that when you search for a specific attraction (such as the Seattle Space Needle), you get only the Seattle Space Needle. However, that's too simple. Google Map gives you several choices. Tap the "B" to get more detailed results (as shown in Figure 12-7).

Figure 12-7: A street map search
result.

To get directions, tap the Turn Right sign. This brings up the pop-up screen
shown in Figure 12-8.

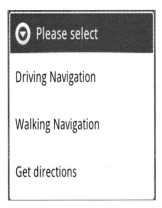

Figure 12-8: Direction options, from
original location to the target.

This gives the options of

✓ **Driving Navigation:** Turn-by-turn directions as you drive from where you are to the destination

✓ **Walking Navigation:** Turn-by-turn directions as you walk to your destination

✓ **Get Directions:** Sequential directions, as shown in Figure 12-9, but without telling you when to turn

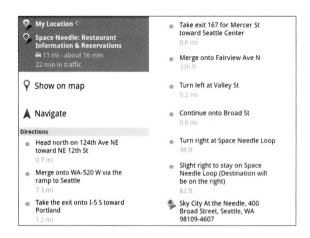

Figure 12-9: Step-by-step directions to the target.

Letting Others Know Where You Are

The Maps application can let you know where you are, but there are also situations where either you want your location to be shared with others or others insist on knowing where you are. For example, you might want to let friends know your location when you're planning to meet at an amusement park. Likewise, parents might insist on knowing the location of their children as a condition for having a cellular phone.

Your Samsung Galaxy S supports these capabilities with the Google Latitude application. This app might or might not be on your phone. It is readily available from Android Market for free, though; see Chapter 9.

Before you can see the location of anyone besides yourself, you have to invite that person. The process is as follows:

1. **Open the Google Maps app.**

   This brings up a map (refer to Figure 12-2).

2. **Tap the Latitude icon, to launch the Latitude service.**

   The Latitude screen opens, as shown in Figure 12-10.

Figure 12-10: The home Latitude screen.

3. **Tap the icon with the combo plus sign/silhouette (top right).**

   This allows you to invite others to be tracked by you. The Add Friends options are shown in Figure 12-11.

4. **Tap the Select from Contacts hyperlink to invite friends or family from your contact list.**

   Tapping this icon brings up all your contacts, as shown in Figure 12-12.

5. **Tap the check box next to the friends you would like to track and then tap the Add Friends button.**

   An e-mail is sent to each contact that you check marked, asking whether that person wants to participate. If and when those folks accept, you can track their location.

Figure 12-11: The Add Friends Latitude invitation options screen.

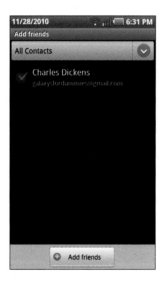

Figure 12-12: Contacts in Latitude.

13

Playing Music and Videos

In This Chapter

▶ Getting the right equipment

▶ Knowing your licensing options

▶ Enjoying a single song, podcasts, or an entire album

▶ Viewing videos

*M*ost smartphones have built-in digital music players. And having a single device that you can use as a phone and serve as a source of entertainment is quite convenient because then, you need only one device rather than two, and you eliminate cords for charging and separate headphones for listening. Your Samsung Galaxy S is no exception. You can play digital music files and podcasts all day and all night on your phone.

In addition, by virtue of the Super AMOLED screen on your Galaxy S smartphone, your phone makes for an excellent handheld video player. Just listen on the headset and watch on the screen, whether you have a short music video or a full-length movie.

To boot, your Galaxy S phone comes with applications for downloading and listening to music as well as downloading and watching video. These apps are very straightforward, especially if you've ever used a CD or a DVD player. In a sense, they're even easier than using a VCR — no need to set the clock!

Carrier Quirks

The only possible pitfall for you playing music and videos is that each carrier has its own spin: Some cellular carriers want you to use their music store, and some give you the freedom to enjoy the flexibility that comes with owning an Android-based phone. You can use the basic multimedia tools that come with the phone, or download the myriad of options that you have via Android Market. (Read all about Market in Chapter 9.)

However, other cellular carriers, and Samsung, offer you the Samsung Media Hub, an all-in-one tool for managing your multimedia options, which I discuss at the end of this chapter.

To keep things straight, read on to see your options regardless of what cellular carrier you use, including the use of the basic multimedia applications that came with your phone. Then, I talk about some of the unique offers for the Verizon Captivate phone model. I wrap up talking about the Samsung Media Hub.

Remember, the whole point is about enjoyment. Enjoy yourself!

Getting Ready to Be Entertained

Regardless of the model phone that you have, for the app you use for entertainment — and whether you're listing to audio or video — here are some common considerations I need to cover up front.

The first is the use of headsets. Yeah, you use *headphones* with your MP3 player, but your phone uses a *headset.* The vocabulary is more than just semantics, too, because a headset has headphones plus a microphone so you can make and take phone calls.

Secondly, you need to know about connecting your Galaxy S phone to a television and/or stereo. After I talk about that, I cover the issue of licensing multimedia material.

Choosing your headset options

You can use wired or wireless (Bluetooth) headsets with your Samsung Galaxy S phone. Wired headsets are less expensive than Bluetooth headsets, and of course, wired headsets don't need charging, as do the Bluetooth headsets.

On the other hand, you lose freedom of mobility if you're tangled up in wires. And, the battery within Bluetooth headsets lasts much longer than the battery of your phone.

Wired headsets

At the top of your Galaxy S phone is a headset jack. If you try to use your regular headphone jack in this jack, it will work, but you can't talk on a call because the headphone doesn't come with a microphone.

Your phone might come with a wired headset. In that case, just plug it in to use the device. This version uses ear buds, like the image shown in Figure 13-1.

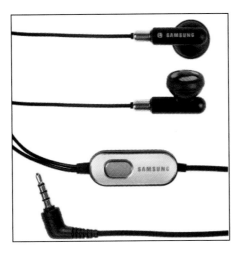

Figure 13-1: A typical wired headset with ear buds and a 3.5mm plug.

Some people dislike ear buds. You can obtain other styles at a number of retail franchises that offer the following options including

- Around-the-ear headphones that place the speakers on the ear and are held in place with a clip
- A behind-the-neck band that holds around-the-ear headphones in place
- An over-the-head band that places the headphones on the ear

The laws in some regions prohibit the use of headphones while driving. Correcting the officer and explaining that these are really "headsets," and not "headphones" won't help your case if you're pulled over. Even if not explicitly illegal in an area, it's still a bad idea to play music in both ears at a volume that inhibits your ability to hear warnings while driving.

In any case, give it some time to get used to any new headset. There is often an adjustment period while you get used to having a foreign object in or around your ear.

Stereo Bluetooth headsets

The other option is to use a stereo Bluetooth headset. Figure 13-2 shows a typical model.

A stereo Bluetooth headset is paired the same way as any other Bluetooth headset. (Read how to do this in Chapter 3.) When your Galaxy S phone and the headset connect, the phone recognizes that it operates in stereo when listening to music or videos.

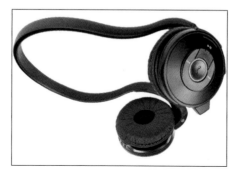

Figure 13-2: A behind-the-neck Bluetooth stereo headset.

There are also several variations on how to place the headphone part of the headset near your ear with a Bluetooth headset. Be aware that some products on the market are strictly Bluetooth headphones, and not headsets. This means that they don't have a microphone to allow you to answer a phone call. In this case, you might want to remove your headphones when a call comes in.

Connecting to your stereo or TV

You can connect your Galaxy S phone to your stereo. If you have a Verizon Fascinate or an AT&T Captivate model, you can also connect your phone to your TV. The RCA connector cable shown in Figure 13-3 shows the cable with the 3.5mm plug that fits into the headset jack on your phone.

Figure 13-3: The cable with a 3.5mm plug and RCA connectors.

Connecting to your stereo

Although being able to listen to your music on the move is convenient, it's also nice to be able to listen to your music collection on your home stereo. Your Galaxy S phone presents your stereo with a nearly perfect version of what went in. The sound quality that comes out is limited only by the quality of your stereo.

In addition, you can play the music files and playlists stored on your phone, which can be more convenient than playing CDs. Setting this up involves plugging the 3.5mm jack from the cable in Figure 13-3 into the phone and inserting the red and white color-coded RCA jacks into the red and white jacks on your stereo. (The yellow plug can just hang loose.) When you play the music as you do through a headset, it will play through your stereo. You will be entertained.

Connecting to your TV

You can also play videos from your phone on your TV — if you have an AT&T Captivate or a Verizon Fascinate model — by following these steps:

1. **On your TV, plug the color-coded RCA connectors on the cable in Figure 13-3 to your TV.**

   The red plug goes into the red jack on the TV, the white plug goes into the white jack, and the yellow plug goes into the yellow jack. It doesn't matter which order you plug these in.

2. **Turn on the TV and make sure that it's set to the channel for the jacks that you're using.**

   For example, your cable box might be in video input #1, and you have plugged into video input #2. This is often controlled by the channel changer on the TV.

3. **Go to your phone and plug the 3.5mm plug from the cable in Figure 13-3 into the headset jack.**

4. **From the Home screen on your phone, tap the Application list icon.**

5. **Flick or pan to the Settings icon and tap it.**

6. **Tap the Sound and Display icon.**

   A long list of settings opens. Toward the bottom is the TV Out option.

7. **Tap the TV Out check box.**

   This tells the phone to start sending video signals to the headset jack. Most of the time, it doesn't bother.

   You should now see and hear everything that takes place on your phone on your TV. Start the video application and enjoy! I show you how to use the Video Player application later in this chapter.

Your phone can't switch mid-video from playing on your phone to playing on your TV. If you happen to be in the middle of your movie, you need to shut down the Video Player application and restart the app and the movie.

Licensing your multimedia files

It's really quite simple: You need to pay the artist to listen to music or watch video with integrity. Many low-cost options are suitable for any budget. Depending upon how much you plan to listen to music, podcasts, or watch videos, you can figure out what's the best deal.

Stealing music or videos is uncool. Although it might be technically possible to play pirated music and videos on your phone, it's stealing. Don't do it.

You can buy or lease them to acquire music, podcasts, or videos. In most cases, you pay for them with a credit card. And depending upon your cellular carrier, you might be allowed to pay for them on your monthly cellular bill.

Listening up on licensing

Here are the three primary licensing options available for music files and podcasts:

- **By the track:** Pay for each song individually. Buying a typical song costs about 79 to 99 cents. Podcasts, which are frequently used for speeches or lectures, can vary dramatically in price.

- **By the album:** Buying an album isn't a hold-over from the days before digital music. Music artists and producers create albums with the organization of songs to offer a consistent feeling or mood. Although many music-playing applications allow you to assemble your own playlist, an album is created by professionals. In addition, buying a full album is often less expensive than on a per-song basis. You can get multiple songs for $8 to $12.

- **With a monthly pass:** The last option for buying audio files is the monthly pass. For about $15 per month, you can download as much music as you want from the library of the service provider.

If you let your subscription lapse with a monthly pass provider, these services are set up so that you can't listen to the music from this library.

In addition to full access to the music library, some music library providers offer special services to introduce you to music that's similar to what you've been playing. These services are a very convenient way to learn about new music. If you have even a small interest in expanding your music repertoire, these services are an easy way to do it.

Whether buying or renting is most economical depends on your listening/ viewing habits. If you don't plan to buy much, or you know specifically what you want, you might save some money by paying for all your files individually. If you're not really sure what you want, or you like a huge variety of things, paying for monthly access might make better sense for you.

Licensing for videos

The two primary licensing options available for videos are

- **Rental:** This option is similar to renting a video from a store. You can view the video as many times as you like within 24 hours from the start of the first play. In addition, the first play must begin within a defined period, such as a week, of your downloading it. When you rent, you have two resolution options, depending on which device you intend to play the video:

  - *SD (standard definition) resolution:* This lower-cost rental uses a smaller file. SD is fine if you're going to run the video only on your phone or your non-HD TV. An SD-resolution rental costs about $4 or $5. This is the format that works fine when you download videos for viewing on your phone.

  - *HD (high definition) resolution:* Yeah, you *can* choose this option and pay a higher price, but it does you no good. The screen on your phone and the video output are SD resolution.

- **Purchase:** You have a license to view the file as frequently as you want, for as long as you want. The purchase cost can be as low as $12, but is more typically in the $15 range.

At the moment, there are no sources for mainstream Hollywood films that allow you to buy a monthly subscription and give you unlimited access to their film library. This can change at any time, so watch for announcements.

Enjoying Basic Multimedia Capabilities

Regardless of the version of your Galaxy S, some basic multimedia capabilities are common across the different phones. Figure 13-4 shows a typical Application list with multimedia options.

Your phone comes with the Music Player and Video Player applications preloaded, and you might have other multimedia applications as well, depending upon the model.

Multimedia apps

Figure 13-4: The Application list, showing multimedia apps.

Don't worry about storage capacity for your music. A very rough estimate is that a gigabyte (GB) of storage will store 100 hours of music. The memory cards that come with your phone can store several gigabytes. You can also buy memory cards these days that can store 32GB. There are limits on storing videos, though. Roughly, one full-length movie takes up 1GB. Don't try to put your entire video collection on your phone.

Grooving with the Music Player app

The Music Player app allows you to play music and audio files. The first step is to obtain music and audio files for your phone.

Ways to acquire music and/or recordings for your phone are

- ✔ Buy and download tracks from an online music store.
- ✔ Load them on your MicroSD memory card from the digital music collection on your PC.
- ✔ Receive them as an attachment via e-mail or text message.
- ✔ Receive them from another device connected with a Bluetooth link.
- ✔ Record on your phone.

Buying from an online music store

The most straightforward method of getting music on your phone is from an online music store. You can download a wide variety of music from dozens of mainstream online music stores. Better-known sites include Rhapsody, Amazon MP3, MP3.com, and Walmart.

In addition, many more specialty or "boutique" stores provide more differentiated offerings than you can get from the mass-market stores. For example, MAQAM offers Middle Eastern music (www.maqammp3.com).

The details for acquiring music among the online stores vary from store to store. Ultimately, there are more similarities than differences. As an example of when you know what you want, what you really, really want, here's how to find and download the song "Wannabe" sung by the Spice Girls. I'm using Amazon MP3. If you don't have Amazon MP3 in your Application list, you would start by loading that app on your phone, as I describe in Chapter 9. When you open it, you see the screen shown in Figure 13-5.

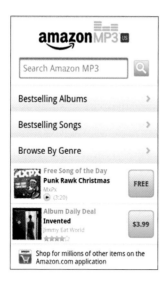

Figure 13-5: The Amazon MP3 Home screen.

From here, you can search for music by album, song, or music genre. Amazon MP3 offers a different free music track and an album at a deep discount every day.

Now to search for the song you want.

1. **Enter the relevant search information in the Amazon MP3 Search field.**

   In this case, I'm searching for "Wannabe" by the Spice Girls. The result of the search for songs looks like Figure 13-6.

Figure 13-6: Search results for a song at the Amazon MP3 store.

2. **To purchase the track, tap twice on the price.**

   The left screen in Figure 13-7 shows the price. When you tap once on the price, you get a confirmation message to be sure that you want to buy the download; the price is replaced with a Buy icon, as shown on the right in Figure 13-7. To buy, tap Buy.

3. **Sign in with your account information, as shown in Figure 13-8.**

   Unless you're going to subsist on the free MP3 files you can get from this site, you need to pay. To pay for files at an online music store, you need an account and a credit card. This process is similar, if not identical, to signing up for Android Market (see Chapter 9). You need your e-mail account, password, and in some cases, an account name. In the case of Amazon MP3, you already have an account if you have an account with Amazon. If not, you'll be asked to create an account.

Figure 13-7: Tap twice to buy.

Figure 13-8: The account sign-in
screen for the Amazon MP3 store.

After you enter this information, the file will automatically begin downloading to your phone, and a progress screen (as shown in Figure 13-9)
lets you know when you're finished.

The song is now loaded on your phone. When you open the music
player, it is ready for you to play.

Figure 13-9: Downloading screen for tracks from the Amazon MP3 store.

Loading digital music from your PC

In addition to acquiring music files from an online music store, you can also transfer digital music tracks stored on your PC.

The challenge is choosing the method to transfer files from your PC to your phone. If you plan to download one or a few files, using e-mail is most convenient. (The next section covers receiving music files via e-mail as an attachment.) If you plan to move a large music library from your PC to your phone, though, the e-mail approach is too cumbersome. Instead, load the memory card that resides within your phone by connecting it to your PC.

You'll need to use an adapter — a card reader — that allows you to insert your MicroSD memory card in a holder with a standard USB connection. An image of one such adapter with the memory card is in Figure 13-10. The actual size of the card is about as big as the fingernail on your pinky.

Each model of phone has an SD card that comes with it. You can buy cards with larger capacity if you wish. Prices for these memory cards have been dropping, but as a ballpark, a 4GB card will run you $5, $10 for 8GB, $22 for 16GB, and $76 for 32GB. Expect to pay more at a cellular carrier's retail store, though.

Figure 13-10: A MicroSD card and a USB adapter.

If you've ever used a thumb drive to transfer a file from one PC to another, you'll find the process similar when you're copying music files to your phone via the MicroSD card. These steps are as follows:

1. **Turn off your phone.**

2. **Remove the back of your phone, as described in Chapter 2.**

3. **Remove the MicroSD card from your phone.**

   The memory card lies flat in its slot. To remove it, use a fingernail to push it in further into its slot. The spring will eject it slightly from the slot.

4. **Insert your memory card into your adapter.**

5. **Plug your adapter into your PC.**

   When you plug in the USB-MicroSD Adapter into a USB port, your PC recognizes it as just another thumb drive (a removable disk) and queries you as to what you want to do. A typical choice pop-up menu for a PC is shown in Figure 13-11. The actual screen you see depends upon how your PC is set up, of course.

6. **Click Open Folder to View Files.**

   This opens a window with the files on your MicroSD card.

7. **On your PC, open the folder with your digital music, and copy the files you want to your MicroSD card.**

   Don't worry about which folder to place the files. Your phone is happy to do that for you.

Figure 13-11: A typical AutoPlay
pop-up screen on a PC.

8. **After all the files are copied, eject the adapter-MicroSD card from your PC.**

9. **Remove the MicroSD card from your adapter and put it back in your phone.**

10. **Turn on your phone.**

    Your phone sees these new files, knows that they are audio files, and organizes them for you when you open up the Music Player app. Done.

You might have a program on your PC that manages your digital music files. For example, SanDisk Media Manager is a PC application that automates much of the transfer of files for Steps 7 and 8. If you have such a PC application, by all means, use it. Let it do the heavy lifting for you.

Receiving music as an attachment

As long as you comply with your license agreement, you can e-mail or text a music file as an attachment to anyone, including yourself. Simply send yourself an e-mail from your PC with the desired music file. You then open the e-mail and text on your phone, as shown in Figure 13-12.

Your phone can play music files that come in any of the following formats: FLAC, WAV, Vorbis, MP3, AAC, AAC+, eAAC+, WMA, AMR-NB, AMR-WB, MID, AC3, and XMF.

All you need to do is tap Save, and the file is saved on your phone and accessible from the Music Player app. Done.

Figure 13-12: An e-mail with an attached music file.

Recording sounds on your phone

No one else might think your kids' rendition of "Happy Birthday" is anything special, but you probably treasure it. In fact, there are many recording apps that you can obtain if your phone didn't come with one.

In general, there is a simple record button that creates a sound file when you stop recording. The sound quality might not be the best, but what you record can be just as important or entertaining as what you buy commercially. Your phone treats all audio files the same and is playable on your Music Player.

Playing downloaded music

To play your music, open the Music Player application; refer to Figure 13-4. Just tap that icon. The first screen that you see sorts your music files into a number of categories, as shown in Figure 13-13.

Figure 13-13: Music categories for the Music Player app.

The categories include

- ✔ **All:** This lists all your song files in alphabetical order.

- ✔ **Playlists:** Some digital music stores bundle songs into playlists, such as Top Hits from the 50s. You can also create your own playlists for groups of songs that are meaningful to you.

- ✔ **Albums:** Tapping this category places all your songs into an album with which the song is associated. When you tap the album, you see all the songs you've purchased, whether one song or all the songs from that album, as shown in Figure 13-14.

Figure 13-14: Albums sort for the Music Player app.

- ✔ **Artists:** This category takes all songs from all the albums from a given artist and lists it here.

- ✔ **Genres:** This category separates music into music genres, such as country and western, or heavy metal.

These categories are useful when you have a large number of files. To play a song, an album, or a genre, open that category and tap the song, playlist, album, artist, or genre, and the song will start playing.

Adding songs as ringtones and alarms

Here's how to add a song as a ringtone or alarm. While the song is playing, tap the Menu button to bring up a menu like that shown in Figure 13-15.

Figure 13-15: Menu options while playing music in the Music Player app.

Tap Set As to bring up the pop-up menu shown in Figure 13-16.

You have three very convenient options:

- **Voice Call Ringtone:** Replace the default ring sound with this song when receiving a call.

- **Caller Ringtone:** Assign this song or audio file to ring when you receive a call from a certain person in your Contacts list on your phone.

- **Alarm Tone:** Have your phone play this song for a saved alarm.

Figure 13-16: Music Player app Set As options.

Creating playlists

To create a playlist or add to a playlist, tap the Menu button when a song is playing. Tap the More option and then tap Add to Playlist. Select a playlist you want to add this song to or create a new playlist.

Figure 13-17 shows a list of playlists. If you want to add that song to an existing playlist, you tap that name of that playlist, and it's added. And the next time you select that playlist, it's there.

If you want to create a new playlist, you're asked to name it. Make it meaningful to you, like "Favorites from 2010" or "Children's songs." You can add as many songs to a playlist as you like.

Jamming to Internet radio

If you have not tried Internet radio, it is definitely worth considering. The basic idea is that you enter information on your current music favorites, and these services will play music that is similar. Pandora and Slacker Radio are two of the best known services of this type and one or the other may be preloaded on your phone. If not, they are available for download from Android Market (see Chapter 9).

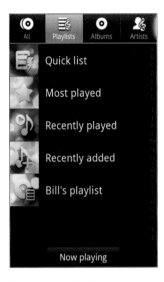

Figure 13-17: Playlists on my phone.

These are a great way to learn about new songs and groups that may appeal to you. The service will stream music to your phone for you to enjoy. You can buy tracks if you choose.

Streaming audio files uses a large amount of data over time. This may be no problem if you have an unlimited data service plan. Otherwise, your "free" Internet radio service can wind up costing you a lot.

Looking at your video options

The Music Player app allows you to play music files. Similarly, you use the Video Player to play video options. The Video Player is in your Application list and might even be on your home page. In most ways, playing videos is the same as playing audio with a few exceptions:

- ✔ Many people prefer to buy music, but renting is more typical for videos.
- ✔ Video files are usually, but not always, larger.

Otherwise, similar to music files, you can acquire videos for your phone from an online video store, and you need to have an account and pay for the use. In addition, you can download video files to your phone, and the Video Player will play them like a VCR or DVD player.

In Chapter 10, I cover how to use the digital camcorder on your phone. You can watch any video you've shot on your phone from the Video Player application.

An important difference between the Music Player and the Video Player is that the video files aren't categorized. As shown in Figure 13-18, the files are listed in rank order by type.

Figure 13-18: List of videos for the Video Player app.

You can rank videos by size, name, date, and type (format) by tapping the menu. That's as sophisticated as this application will get.

Your phone can show the following video formats: MPEG-4, WMV, AVI/DivX, MKV, and FLV.

To play your video, simply tap the name of the file, as shown in Figure 13-18. The app begins showing the video in landscape orientation. The controls that pop up when you tap the screen are similar to a VCR or DVD player.

Navigating Other Multimedia Apps

Depending upon your cellular carrier, other multimedia services are preloaded on your phone. The Fascinate is preloaded with a service from Verizon called V CAST. The other Galaxy S phones are preloaded with a service from Samsung called Media Hub.

V CAST on the Verizon Fascinate

Verizon offers the V CAST service for all its customers with multimedia-capable phones. V CAST Music, as the name implies, offers downloadable music. What you download is charged on your Verizon bill.

The home screen for V CAST Music is shown in Figure 13-19.

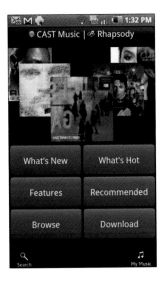

Figure 13-19: The V CAST Music Home screen.

The cost per song here is $1.99. This is somewhat more costly than other services, but there is the convenience of direct billing through Verizon.

Similarly, V CAST Video offers videos in a number of formats. These include news, sports, and TV shows in addition to full-length movies. Depending upon the selection, the images are "streamed" to your phone or downloaded.

Video streaming is a technology where your phone receives and displays the video but doesn't store it. This is like how your television works. Such an approach works well with news and sports broadcasts.

You and I are usually indifferent to whether video is downloaded or streamed unless you happen to want to watch the video a second time or are in an area with spotty or no cellular coverage. V CAST Video lets you know whether the video is streamed video when you look at the descriptions of the video.

Both V CAST Music and V CAST Video use the existing multimedia applications on the phone. You can play the music or downloaded videos by launching your Music Player or Video Player app.

Samsung Media Hub

In the latter part of 2010, Samsung began rolling out its Media Hub offering for the Sprint Epic 4G, the T-Mobile Vibrant, and the AT&T Captivate. This video storefront presents a selection of digital videos that you can rent or buy.

The three primary areas are

- **My Media:** Videos that you've downloaded
- **Movie Store:** Major motion pictures to rent or buy
- **TV Store:** Video file downloads of popular television episodes

As with other digital stores, you need to provide an e-mail address, a password, and a credit card to access these videos. They are then downloaded to your phone.

You can connect up to five devices to each account, allowing you to share downloads across multiple devices. In addition, Samsung Smart TVs can access Media Hub. This means you'll be able to finish a movie you started watching on your phone on your Samsung big-screen when you get home.

The licensing of some videos does not allow for their display on a large screen TV. This is unfortunate. What is also unfortunate is that you do not get a message like "This video is not licensed for display on a large screen TV." Instead, you get the message, "TV-Out not supported while application running. Phone display only." The key message is "Phone display only."

Part V
Productivity Applications

The 5th Wave   By Rich Tennant

"What I'm doing should clear your sinuses, take away your headache, and charge your Samsung Galaxy S."

In this part . . .

*A*ccess to business information when you're mobile makes you more productive. Without the weight and hassle of carrying a laptop, you can be set up to access real-time company information. In addition to reviewing these data, you can make updates to and customize information for clients.

Among the most commonly used tools in most business environments is your electronic calendar. In this part, I tell you how to make additions, changes, and deletions to your electronic business calendar from your Galaxy S phone.

Sure, you can have a lot of fun with your Galaxy S phone . . . but you can get a lot done with it, too, and in this part, I show you how. I also show you how to work on Microsoft Office documents and spreadsheets through the ThinkFree app.

Using the Calendar

*Y*ou might fall in love with your Galaxy S phone so much that you want to ask it out on a date. And speaking of dates, the subject of this chapter is the calendar on your phone. The Galaxy S phone Calendar functions are cool and powerful, and they can make your life easier. And with just a few taps, you can bring all your electronic calendars together to keep your life synchronized.

In this chapter, I show you how to set up the calendar that comes with your phone, which might be all you need. The odds are, though, that you have calendars elsewhere, such as on your work computer. So, I also show you how to integrate all your calendars with your Galaxy S phone. After you read this chapter, you'll have no excuse for missing a meeting.

Some calendars use the term "appointments" for "events." Samsung uses events, so that's the term I use.

Syncing Calendars

Most likely, you already have at least two electronic calendars scattered in different places: a calendar tied to your work computer and a personal calendar synced to Gmail. Now, you have a third one to maintain with your Samsung phone.

You may already be a winner!

The calendar on your phone might already be populated with events from your work and personal calendars. Don't be concerned — this is good news!

If you've already set up your phone to sync with your e-mail and your calendar (see Chapter 6),

your calendars are already synchronizing with your phone. Tap the Menu button, then the Settings icon to find a list of the calendars that sync to your phone.

Bringing together all your electronic calendars to one place, though, is one of the best things about your phone — as long as you're a faithful user of your electronic calendars, that is. To begin this process, you need to provide authorization to the respective places that your calendars are stored. This authorization is necessary to respect your privacy.

If your phone doesn't have a Calendar shortcut on the home page, open the Calendar app from your App list. This same app works with the calendar that's stored on your phone and any digital calendars that you add.

When you first open this app, you see a calendar in monthly format, as shown in Figure 14-1. I discuss other calendar views later in this chapter.

Figure 14-1: The monthly calendar display.

Follow these steps to tell your phone to sync with another calendar:

1. **From any of the calendar display screens, including the one shown in Figure 14-1, tap the Menu button, of the Device Function keys.**

2. **Tap the Settings icon.**

   The Settings screen appears, as shown in Figure 14-2.

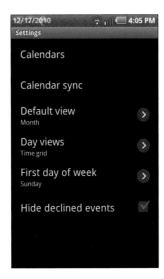

Figure 14-2: The Calendar Settings menu.

3. **Tap the Calendar Sync hyperlink.**

   The General Sync Settings screen appears, as shown in Figure 14-3.

   All the calendars synced to your phone are listed under the Manage Accounts section.

4. **Make sure that the Background Data and the Auto-Sync check boxes are selected.**

   I explain more about synchronization options later in this section. For now, just make sure that these two check boxes are selected.

5. **Tap the Add Account button.**

   The screen shown in Figure 14-4 appears for you to add a calendar.

Figure 14-3: The Calendar sync options.

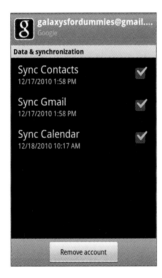

Figure 14-4: Account sync options.

6. Tap the Sync Calendar hyperlink.

The assumption with your Galaxy S phone is that your digital calendar is associated with an e-mail service. This means that synching your phone follows the process that's practically identical to adding e-mail. This screen allows you to select which services to sync. In most cases, you want to sync all options at the same time.

After you set this preference, all the information on the account — including your calendar, e-mail, and contacts — will be updated accordingly.

As I note earlier, the two options for setting synchronization options, as shown in Figure 14-3, are

- ✔ Background Data
- ✔ Auto-sync

In general, it's most convenient to select both of these options. When both are enabled, your phone — without prompting from you — will contact (via the Internet) the computer where you store your e-mail, contacts, and digital calendar to look for any updates. Your phone does this with all the services that you've registered through your phone.

This polling will take place about every hour if you're not actively using your phone. If you're sending e-mail, adding contacts, or changing your calendar while on your phone, your phone will immediately update your service.

Other than the calendar stored on your phone, the Calendar application is simply displaying the information that it gets from a remote calendar. The Calendar app will send the updates to your calendar when you make changes. However, it checks in on your remote calendar only every hour — and only if you set it up to do so.

You could encounter scheduling conflicts if others can create events for you on your digital calendar. Be aware of this possibility. It can be annoying or worse when you have a free time slot when talking to someone, offer it to that person, and then find that someone at the office took it. You can avoid this problem by manually synching your calendar before you tell someone you have a time slot free. I explain how to do this later in this chapter.

Using Auto-sync

Every time your phone polls the service, your phone is sending and receiving data, even if there are no changes. It doesn't take much battery to do this, but it does add up. An option to save some battery life is that you can clear the Auto-sync option.

That way, the phone syncs only when you take an action — such as create a new e-mail, contact, or event — or you manually tell the phone to sync. *Note:* You need to be in the Email app to manually sync.

To change this process, open your e-mail account as discussed in Chapter 6. When you see your e-mails, press the Menu button and then tap Refresh.

Using Background Data

The other option you can enable (or not) is Background Data. Having the sync process operate in the background allows you to do other things. If you clear this option, you cannot do other things. In addition, of course, you can't use Auto-sync if you clear this option. My recommendation: Go ahead and leave this one checked.

Setting Calendar Display Preferences

Before you get too far playing around with your calendar, you'll want to choose how you view it.

If you don't have a lot of events on your calendar, using the monthly display shown in Figure 14-1 is probably a fine option. On the other hand, if your day is jam-packed with personal and professional events, the daily or weekly schedules might prove more practical. Switching views is easy. For example, just tap the Week button at the top of the calendar to show the weekly display, as shown in Figure 14-5.

Figure 14-5: The weekly calendar display.

Or, tap the Day button at the top of the calendar to show the daily display, as shown in Figure 14-6.

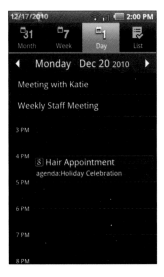

Figure 14-6: The daily calendar display.

The "g" icon to the left of the name of an event (Hair Appointment, in this figure) means that this event is stored on the calendar of a Google Gmail account.

To see what events you have upcoming, regardless of the day they're on, you might prefer list view. Tap the List button at the top of the calendar to see a list of your activities, as shown in Figure 14-7.

Changing the default view

You can change the default view from monthly so that when you open the Calendar app, you see exactly the view you want. From one of the calendar display screens, follow these steps to set your default view:

1. **Tap the Menu button, of the Device Function keys.**

2. **Tap the Settings Button.**

   This brings up the Calendar Settings menu shown in Figure 14-2.

3. **Tap Default View.**

   This brings up your options shown in Figure 14-8.

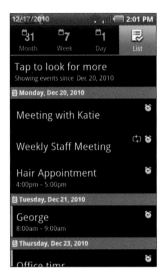

Figure 14-7: List calendar display.

Figure 14-8: The Default View pop-up screen.

4. **Tap the default option you want.**

The next time you open your calendar, the default option automatically comes up.

Setting other display options

In addition to the default display option, you can set other personal preferences, shown in Figure 14-2, for the calendar on your phone. Your phone might or might not have all these options.

- **Calendars:** A list of the calendars that you've set up to work with your phone.

- **Calendar Sync:** Your sync options, as described earlier in this chapter.

- **Day Views:** Daily calendar set to show events on an hour-by-hour grid (showing events and the unscheduled times) or as just a list of sequential events. You can select either option.

- **First Day of Week:** Which day of the week shows first. Most calendars start with Sunday as the first day of the week, but some users prefer to set other days of the week as the first (think Manic Monday). The default is Sunday, but this option allows you to set your preference to any day of the week.

- **Hide Declined Events:** If available, the option to see events that you've declined. The default is to not show these, but if you do want to see them, clear this check box.

- **Calendar Notification:** If available, have events pop up on your notification screen. You can enable or disable this option.

- **Select Ringtone:** If you enable the option to get notifications of events, you can use the Select Ringtone option to play an audio file to announce that its time has arrived.

- **Vibrate:** Similarly, if you enable the option to get notifications of events, you can have the phone vibrate to announce that it's time for the next event.

- **Backup Assistant:** The Verizon Fascinate allows you to set up a service that will automatically back-up the information on your phone.

Creating an Event on the Right Calendar

An important step in using a calendar when mobile is creating an event. It is even more important to make sure that it ends up on the right calendar.

Creating, editing, and deleting an event

Here's how to create an event — referred to as an "event" — on your phone. Start from one of the calendar displays shown in Figures 14-1, 14-5, 14-6, or 14-7.

1. **Tap the Menu button, of the Device Function keys.**

2. **Tap the Create icon.**

   This brings up the screen shown in Figure 14-9.

Figure 14-9: The Create Event screen.

3. **Enter the information into the appropriate fields.**

   The only required information is the event name and the To and From dates and start/end times.

You need the following information at hand when making an event:

   ✔ **Event:** A name that you'll remember.

   ✔ **Calendar:** Which calendar you want to keep this event. The My Calendar option in Figure 14-9 would save the event to your phone. When you tap this selection, the phone will present you with the other calendars you have synced to your phone, where you can store an event.

   ✔ **From and To:** The two entry fields for the date and the start and end times.

If you want, you can enter more details on the meeting by scrolling down the Create Event screen and adding

- ✔ **Location:** 'Nuff said.

- ✔ **Alarm:** You can have an alarm at the time of the event, or it can warn you a few minutes in advance.

- ✔ **Repeat:** This option is useful for recurring events, such as weekly meetings.

- ✔ **Description:** Add information that you find useful about that meeting.

After you fill in the obligatory and any optional fields and settings, tap Save. The event is stored in whichever calendar you selected. If you opt for Auto-sync and the event is to be saved other than within the calendar on your phone, your phone will let the selected service know about this event.

After you save an event, you can edit or delete it:

- ✔ **Edit:** Open the event by tapping it from within one of the calendar views. Then, tap the Menu icon. This brings up the option to edit your event. Make your changes and tap Save. It's changed — *if* you have Auto-sync enabled.

- ✔ **Delete:** Open the event by tapping it. Tap the Menu icon. This brings up the option to delete the event. Tap Delete. When a confirmation message appears asking whether you're sure this is what you want to do, tap OK. The event is gone from your phone.

Keeping events separate and private

When you have multiple calendars stored in one place (in this case, your phone), it might get confusing when you want to add a new event. It can be even more confusing when you need to add the real event on one calendar and a placeholder on another.

Say that your boss is a jerk. To retain your sanity, you need to find a new job. You send your resume to the arch-rival firm, Plan B, which has offices across town. Plan B is interested and wants to interview you at 3 p.m. next Tuesday. All good news.

The problem is that your current boss demands that you track your every move on the company calendaring system. His Draconian management style is to berate people if they're not at their desk doing work, if not at a scheduled meeting. (By the way, I am not making up this scenario).

You follow my drift. You don't want Snidely Whiplash trudging through your calendar, sniffing out your plans to exit stage left, and making life more miserable if Plan B doesn't work out. Instead, you want to put a reasonable sounding placeholder on your work calendar, while putting the real event on your personal calendar. You can easily do this from your calendar on your Samsung Galaxy S. When you're making the event, you simply tell the phone where you want the event stored, making sure to keep which event belongs where.

The process begins with the Create Event screen shown in Figure 14-9. The information for the real event is shown in Figure 14-10.

Figure 14-10: The Add an Event screen on your phone.

When you save the event, it's stored strictly on your phone. Now you can create a new event, which in this case is a phony doctor's event, on your work calendar. This time, you open an event, as shown in Figure 14-11.

When you create the event this time, you enter the information you want to be seen on your work calendar. Before you save it, tap the Calendar option. This brings up the screen shown in Figure 14-12.

After you save the event, it will be forever more on that calendar until you delete it. Just be sure to keep straight which calendar you intend to store which event. The name of the calendar on which each event is stored appears under the Calendar heading, as shown in Figures 14-11 and 14-12.

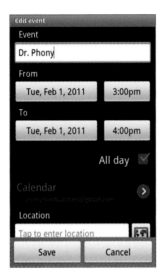

Figure 14-11: The event for your work calendar.

Figure 14-12: Adding an event to your Calendar options.

Now, when you look at your calendar on your phone, you see two events at the same time. Check it out in Figure 14-13. The Galaxy S doesn't mind if you make two simultaneous events.

Figure 14-13: Two events on the same day on your phone calendar.

Under the circumstances, this is what you wanted to create. As long as your boss doesn't see your phone, you're safe — to try to find more fulfilling employment, that is.

Taking Your Work with You

In This Chapter

▶ Using Mobile Office applications

▶ Navigating the Office applications in the Cloud

▶ Sharing files using your phone

*W*hen you pick up your Galaxy S phone, you're holding as much computing power as was available in a high-end laptop five years ago and a graphics processor that would have made a hard-core gamer envious. So it's not far-fetched to want to work on your Microsoft Office applications, which are relatively modest users of computing power, on your Galaxy S while you're away from your desk. Sure. Why not?

There are actually a few good reasons why the Galaxy S phone doesn't allow you to leave your computer behind for good. The most basic is that the sizes of the screen and the keyboard aren't conducive for writing novels and other similarly long documents. What makes the most sense is to have the ability to view Office documents and make minor changes while you are mobile, but to leave the hard-core creation and modification efforts to a full-sized PC.

Sample.docx
4.89KB, 2010-12-16 21:07:2

Sampleppt.ppt
7.50KB, 2010-12-16 21:10:5

Spreadsheet.xls
13.50KB, 2010-12-16 21:10

To support this, Samsung put the power of the ThinkFree Office Mobile for Android on your phone to let you be productive on the road without the need to pull out your laptop. Depending on what you want to do, you might even be able to leave your heavy laptop at home.

In this chapter, I start with an introduction on the basics, explore the tools on your phone, and explain how you can use them to your best advantage. Then I walk you through the ThinkFree Web site so you can know where everything is. Finally, I fill you in on file sharing, so you can get files on and off your phone and out into the world.

Preparing for Using Office Apps

Before I get too far along, I want to explain the capabilities of this solution and the logic behind working with office applications.

Focusing on the Big Four

Microsoft Office applications are the most popular apps for general purpose business productivity. Virtually every business uses Microsoft Office or applications that can interoperate with Microsoft file formats. As you're probably well aware, the heavy hitters are

- **Microsoft Word:** For creating and editing documents. These files use the .txt, .doc, and .docx suffixes. The app in the ThinkFree suite that works with these files is ThinkFree Write.

- **Microsoft Excel:** For managing spreadsheets, performing numerical analysis, and creating charts. These files end in the .xls and .xlsx suffixes. The ThinkFree app that works with these files is ThinkFree Calc.

- **Microsoft PowerPoint:** For creating and viewing presentations. These files end in the .ppt and .pptx suffixes. The ThinkFree app for these files is ThinkFree Show.

In addition to these Microsoft Office apps, the ThinkFree PDF Viewer app allows you to view documents sent in the popular PDF format on your screen.

For everything Microsoft Office, check out *Office 2010 For Dummies* or *Office 2007 For Dummies,* by Wallace Wang (Wiley).

The newest versions of Microsoft Office files are appended with .docx, .xlsx, and .pptx. ThinkFree can work with the older and newer formats, though. In general, more applications work with the older versions. You don't give up much by using the older version, but you do gain more compatibility with other people who aren't as current. Over time, the discrepancies will become less of an issue as more people update to the newer format.

Accessing the Office files

The next challenge in working with Office files is keeping track of the most recent version of whatever file you're working on. The most basic scenario is one in which you're working on a Microsoft Office file yourself. If you have a desktop PC, you're probably accustomed to transferring that file among different machines if you want to work on it in different locations, such as home or work. Here are your traditional options:

- **Removable media:** You use a thumb drive or disc to move the file from one PC to another.

> ✔ **E-mail:** You e-mail the file from one PC to another.
>
> ✔ **Server:** You save a copy of your file from the first PC on a server that you can access from both the first and second PC.

The first option is to use your MicroSD card to transfer files to and from your phone. This process is the same for music files, which I cover in Chapter 13. But you'll probably find this process is not very convenient. This leaves you with the second two options: using e-mail or using a server.

Sending and receiving a Microsoft Office file attachment via a text or e-mail is probably old hat by now. You receive the e-mail, download the attachment, and work away. When you're done, you save the file to work on later, or you send it back to your PC. I go into more details later in this chapter.

The server option calls for a little more explanation. By the way, there is a fancy term for this kind of computing: "cloud computing." Readers of a certain age will recall this computing concept as time-sharing, but that name is out of fashion. "Cloud computing" is in vogue, so this is the terminology I shall use.

Cloud computing

The issue of file sharing is integral to getting the most out of the Office applications on your phone. To make it really work, the more Office files you store on the server, the better. It will do you little good if the files you want to see and change are safely stored on your PC, which you dutifully powered off to save energy.

The principle behind this service is that the server appears to your PC and your phone as if it were a drive or a memory card that's directly connected. If you know how to copy files from, say, your PC hard drive to a USB thumb drive, you can use a server.

When you tap a file that appears on your phone (comparable to double-clicking a file on your PC), the file is opened, and you can read and edit it. What you might not know is what computer is doing the processing. It could be your phone, and it could also be a computer on the server. Ultimately, you don't really care as long as it works fast and does what you want.

When you're done reading or editing, the file gets saved, secure and accessible, until the next time you want to do something to the file. This is the essence of cloud computing, and your phone can happily participate.

ThinkFree offers such a server you can use for cloud computing. You need to sign up with ThinkFree to get access to its server. The good news is that anyone with a Gmail account automatically has a ThinkFree account. Just use your e-mail address and password, and you're set. ThinkFree gives you 1 gigabyte (GB) of storage for your files.

And if you don't want to work with ThinkFree, you have lots of choices. These days, many firms offer you access to a server as a backup service at little or no charge.

For example, one of the more popular cloud computing services in use today is Google Docs (`http://docs.google.com`). With a Gmail account (yet another reason to have such an account), you can upload Office files to the Google Docs server, work on them, and then save the files.

One advantage of using ThinkFree instead of Google Docs is that the ThinkFree app makes it easy to exchange files with your phone. Depending upon your needs, sometimes Internet access isn't available, such as when you're on an airplane. If you want to work on an Office document, you want that file to be stored on your phone.

Reading and Editing Files with Your Phone

The Verizon Fascinate, Sprint Epic 4G, and T-Mobile Vibrant models all come with ThinkFree Mobile Office. Figure 15-1 shows the logo in your Application list.

For most cases, of course, it's unrealistic that a mobile version of a Microsoft Office app would do every capability that you could access on a full, desktop version of Office. But then again, you most likely don't need — or want — a full version of Office on your phone. Reading and some minor editing are all you'll probably do via your phone, and you can easily do these tasks with ThinkFree. *Note:* You can't print from your phone without going through another PC that has Office.

Figure 15-1: The ThinkFree logo.

The AT&T Captivate doesn't come with this app preinstalled, but you can obtain ThinkFree Lite from Android Market for free. This less-beefy version will allow you to view, but not modify, Office documents. You can also buy ThinkFree Office for $14.99 from Android Market. It would have been nice to have this application included on your Captivate, but at least you can solve this problem relatively inexpensively if having this app is important.

Creating a document

To introduce the process, I show you how to create a document on your phone. You can store the doc on your phone or in the cloud.

1. **On your phone, open the Application list and then tap the ThinkFree icon.**

2. **Enter your e-mail address and password.**

3. **Accept the End User License Agreement.**

   You see the Home screen shown in Figure 15-2.

Figure 15-2: The ThinkFree home page on your phone.

4. **Tap the My Docs tab.**

   A folder opens (as shown in Figure 15-3), showing the contents of the MicroSD card and phone memory, and you see whatever files and folders you have there.

5. **Tap the Menu button (of the Device Function keys).**

   This brings up a number of options, as shown in Figure 15-4.

6. **Tap the New icon.**

   This brings up the pop-up screen shown in Figure 15-5.

Figure 15-3: Viewing your ThinkFree My Docs page on your phone.

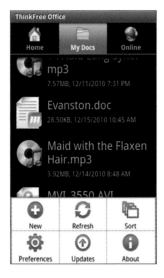

Figure 15-4: The Menu options on the ThinkFree My Docs page.

Figure 15-5: The New Documents choices from the ThinkFree My Docs page.

7. **Tap the type of document you want to create.**

   Sample blank screens for each file format are shown in Figure 15-6.

   - *Document:* Open a blank sheet in Word format (.docx).

   - *Spreadsheet:* Open a blank spreadsheet in Excel spreadsheet format (.xls).

   - *Presentation:* Open a blank presentation in PowerPoint format (.ppt).

   Only true DOC files open in the newer Office format.

   Of course, the new Folder option allows you to create a new folder to provide some order on your MicroSD card.

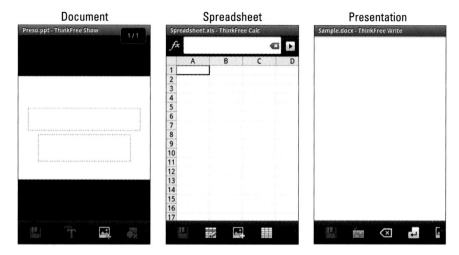

Figure 15-6: Blank documents.

At this point, you can begin to enter text or data.

8. **To save a document, tap the diskette icon (lower left).**

   The diskette might indeed be a relic of PC technology, but it's still widely used to mean Save.

   Your phone saves the document on your MicroSD card in the format you selected.

9. **When prompted, name the document, as shown in Figure 15-7 and then tap OK.**

   The document is stored on your phone.

Figure 15-7: The Save screen for a .docx document.

When you want to find the document again, it will be right where you left it on your phone. You open to the My Docs tab, and find it in the folder where you saved it.

Sending an Office file as an attachment

After a file is saved, it's safe to send it to your home PC or to another PC. When you have the file open and you're ready to e-mail the document to your PC or another PC, follow these steps:

1. **Press the Menu button.**

   You get a pop-up screen, as shown in Figure 15-8.

Figure 15-8: The Menu pop-up for a saved `.docx` document.

2. **Tap the File icon.**

You have several choices from the resulting pop-up screen, as shown in Figure 15-9.

Figure 15-9: File options.

3. **Tap Send.**

   This brings up the options shown in Figure 15-10.

Figure 15-10: Send options.

It is possible to transfer files using Bluetooth radio technology. It's an advanced option that I don't cover in this book.

4. **Tap your e-mail service (such as Gmail).**

   This brings up a blank e-mail screen with your document automatically included as an attachment. This screen is shown in Figure 15-11.

Figure 15-11: The Email screen with your doc set as an attachment.

5. **Populate the To text box with an e-mail address (probably from your contact list), and add a subject and a message if you wish.**

6. **Tap Send.**

   The miracle of wireless communication will zip the document off to the intended recipient.

If you want the document on your PC, simply address it to yourself.

The process is the same for PDF-, Word-, Excel-, and PowerPoint-formatted documents.

The formatting of the document on your phone might not be exactly the same as it is when it reappears on your PC. Save yourself time and don't try to format a document on your Galaxy S phone.

Managing Office documents with a server

Regardless of how you send an Office file to or from your phone, the creation and editing steps are the same. Steps 1–7 of the first step list in the preceding section cover the basics. Although you don't have full access to all the editing tools you find for any of the applications, you can do basic editing with the simplified icons at the bottom of the screen.

The next step is to work with files that you store on a server. As I mention earlier, although you can work with any server, the instructions are easiest when working with the ThinkFree server. The first step is to sign up. The service is free, but ThinkFree wants to know who you are and make sure that you're a real person and not just malware seeking to mess things up. Starting at the ThinkFree home page (refer to Figure 15-2), follow these steps:

1. **Tap the Online tab.**

   This brings up the sign-in screen shown in Figure 15-12.

2. **Tap the Sign Up hyperlink.**

   This brings up a screen similar to that shown in Figure 15-13. I recommend that you use your Gmail account and password, but this is your choice. When completed, you return to the sign-in screen in Figure 15-12.

If you have trouble signing up from your phone, you might have more luck using your PC. The Web site is www.thinkfree.com.

Click here to sign up.

Figure 15-12: The ThinkFree Online page on your phone.

Figure 15-13: The ThinkFree online sign-in screen with security code challenge.

3. **Enter your account name and password, and then tap Sign In.**

4. **(Optional) Have the phone remember your information by selecting the Remember Me check box.**

   Because you haven't had a chance to add anything, the folder will be empty, like that shown in Figure 15-14.

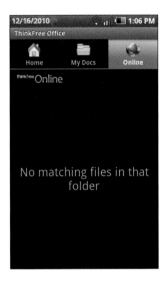

Figure 15-14: You start with an empty folder on the ThinkFree server.

5. **To upload a file from your phone, tap the My Docs tab.**

   This brings up all the files that you have on your phone. Either flick down to the files you want to upload, or open the folder with the files.

6. **Press and hold the file you want to upload from your phone.**

   This brings up the pop-up screen shown in Figure 15-15.

7. **Tap Upload.**

   This brings up a screen like that shown in Figure 15-16. The current files stored on the server will be grayed out.

Figure 15-15: Choose an action here, like uploading.

Figure 15-16: The final upload screen on the ThinkFree server.

8. Tap the Choose button.

This starts to upload the file. After uploading is complete, the file is available on the server and ultimately to your PC, as shown in Figure 15-17.

Figure 15-17: Office Files stored on the ThinkFree server.

Accessing the ThinkFree server from a PC

You can also access the ThinkFree server from a PC:

1. **Enter the ThinkFree Web site from your Web browser.**

   This brings up the sign-in screen shown in Figure 15-18.

Figure 15-18: The ThinkFree online page on a browser.

2. **Sign in with the same user ID and password that you use on your phone with ThinkFree.**

3. **Find your documents on the My Docs tab.**

   From there, you can download or upload files from your PC to your heart's content.

16

The SmartLife Concept

In This Chapter

▶ Getting fast access to popular Internet inquiries

▶ Waking up to the latest information

▶ Enhanced navigation

*U*ser research has shown that four subjects dominate Web searches by smartphone users:

✔ Checking local weather

✔ Getting the latest stock prices

✔ Reading news

✔ Accessing a calendar

A few of these reasons are likely at the top of your priority list when you check your phone. To help you get the most from your phone, Samsung has built into your phone what it calls the "SmartLife" concept in its *Daily Briefing* application, which is essentially a super-widget with which you can quickly customize and bring the information queries to one place.

This chapter covers setting up Daily Briefing. After you have this app set up, Daily Briefing can take care of itself by regularly checking for updates. You just need to do a few taps and swipes when you want to get a quick sense of what's happening around you and out in the world that affects you.

Setting Up Daily Briefing

The Daily Briefing app is preinstalled on your phone. Daily Briefing takes up one full page on the extended home page and consists of a summary for each of its four sections; see Figure 16-1.

✓ Local weather

✓ Stock prices

✓ World news

✓ Your calendar

Perhaps you saw this coming, but these topics correspond to the inquiries that smartphone users access the most.

Figure 16-1: A typical Daily Briefing summary.

To get more info for these topics, tap anywhere on the screen. The Daily Briefing then opens four pages, with a section on the summary page encapsulating each page.

Tap a section on the summary page and you're taken directly to the page that corresponds to the section. For example, if you want more about the local weather, tap the top-most section that shows the basic weather information. Because you tapped the weather summary, it starts by showing a full screen of your local weather page from AccuWeather.com. This full screen is shown in Figure 16-2.

You can scroll to the other three pages of Daily Briefing. The screen to the right of the weather is a page of financial news from Yahoo! Finance. A sample is shown in Figure 16-3.

Figure 16-2: The local weather page in Daily Briefing.

Figure 16-3: Financial news in Daily Briefing.

The world news section comes to the right of the financial news. The information on this screen is provided by AP Mobile News. You can see a sample summary page in Figure 16-4.

Figure 16-4: World news in Daily Briefing.

The fourth and last page is your calendar for today only (in list view), as shown in Figure 16-5.

Figure 16-5: Your daily calendar in Daily Briefing.

The calendar view in Daily Briefing is only for viewing — perfect for when you want to know what you're doing for the day. If you need to make changes to your Calendar, you have to open the Calendar app (see Chapter 14).

To drill down a level on any of these pages, just tap the subject. For example, if you want an hour-by-hour forecast of weather conditions, tap that link on the local weather page.

When you first open Daily Briefing, you won't see as much as what I've shown here. You'll need to customize its pages, and you do this via the Settings menu. Start by tapping the Menu button on any page to bring up the pop-up menu.

Tapping the Setting icon on the pop-up brings up the Settings screen shown in Figure 16-6.

Figure 16-6: The Settings screen in Daily Briefing.

Localizing your weather page

Knowing the weather in Bellevue, WA is very important for some, but if you live in Indianapolis, this information has less value. To change the city for which you receive forecasts, do the following:

1. **Tap the AccuWeather.com link, as shown in Figure 16-6.**

   This brings up the screen shown in Figure 16-7.

Figure 16-7: The weather settings
screen.

2. **Tap the Select City link to bring up the Edit City List screen shown in Figure 16-8.**

   For this example, this screen is populated only with Bellevue.

   Note: When you start, you won't have any cities saved.

3. **To add a city, tap the Add button to bring up the city search screen shown in Figure 16-9.**

   This lists all the major cities for which AccuWeather.com provides forecasts.

4. **When you find the city that you want, tap it.**

   You will get local weather information for this city in addition to all the cities you've already added.

Figure 16-8: City choices for AccuWeather.com.

Figure 16-9: City search screen.

You can add multiple cities at any given time to the Edit City List screen; refer to Figure 16-8 (although it shows just one city). And to delete a city, just highlight its name and then tap the Delete button.

5. **When you're done adding or deleting cities, tap Return until you get back to the Settings screen in Figure 16-6.**

Monitoring the Finance page

From the Yahoo! Finance page, you can monitor the price of stocks or indices delayed by the standard 15-minute lag time that financial news organizations are obligated to use.

1. **Tap the Y! Finance link on the Settings page shown in Figure 16-6; you see a screen like that shown in Figure 16-10.**

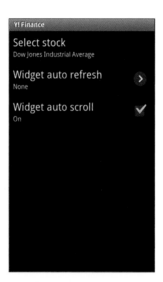

Figure 16-10: The Settings page for Y! Finance in Daily Briefing.

2. **Tap Select Stock to add financial instruments, such as stocks, mutual funds, and stock indices.**

As long as a stock is tracked by Yahoo! Finance, it can be presented. The Select Stock screen shows you the stocks that you're already tracking.

3. **Tap the Add button to add stocks and then enter the name of the stock you're interested in.**

   For example, if you want to add the Russell 2000, tap Add and then enter **Russell 2000** in the search text box, as I show in Figure 16-11.

Figure 16-11: Add what you want to follow via Y! Finance.

   The results then show a list of possibilities for your search.

4. **Select the check box for what you want to see and then tap Save.**

Staying informed on your news page

The news page — top news stories — is presented by AP Mobile News. Your only choices on the setting page, as shown in Figure 16-12, are how often this page is updated and whether the information scrolls. Go ahead, let it scroll. When you see something interesting in the headlines, tap it to go deeper.

I explore synchronization frequency in the next section.

Customizing your calendar

Sorry, but there is nothing for you to do. Whatever is in your calendars for today is already here. Turn to Chapter 14 if you need to make changes to your calendar.

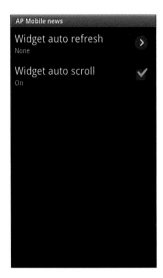

Figure 16-12: The settings page for AP Mobile News.

Setting the Synchronization Frequency

Within each settings screen is a choice as to how frequently you want your phone to access the Internet for the latest update. Each settings screen has a Widget Auto Refresh selection, and the default setting is None.

So, it's up to you to refresh the information shown in Daily Briefing. You do so by tapping the Refresh icon in the bottom-right corner of each page, including the summary Daily Briefing on the extended Home page. This icon is shown in Figure 16-13.

With the default settings, the news feed won't update until and unless you tap the Refresh icon. At that point, your phone accesses the Internet to get the latest information.

To make life more convenient, though, you can have the phone automatically refresh itself at intervals that you set. You can set this interval on the Settings page for each page. For example, when you opt for Widget Auto Refresh (refer to Figure 16-12), you get a pop-up screen like the one shown for Y! Finance in Figure 16-14.

You can select the frequency for a refresh as frequently as every 30 minutes or as infrequently as every three hours.

Refresh button

Figure 16-13: Refresh your Daily Briefing with this icon.

Figure 16-14: The refresh pop-up for Y! Finance.

At first blush, you might wonder why not just set each to the shortest possible duration. The answer is that each query eats battery life. Over time, this constant polling of data can add up.

The lowest power option is to update the screens manually. This takes just a few seconds to get the latest information, and only when you're ready.

If convenience is important, though, go ahead and have each screen automatically update at the least-frequent interval that works for you.

The Other Parts of SmartLife

The notion behind SmartLife is that your Samsung Galaxy S can be integrated into your lifestyle with the net result that you're more connected to the people and issues that are important to you — and spend less time on the boring parts because you're more productive.

Using Daily Briefing speeds your access to the information that other smartphone users need to access by tapping in multiple Web sites. Non-smartphone users have to wait to access this information until they're sitting behind their computer screens.

Likewise, two key accessories allow you to get more from your phone: the home cradle and the car cradle. For a plain old cellphone, a charging cradle is a luxury one might afford oneself. While still a luxury, there is more value to these accessories when you use the cradles with your Galaxy S.

A charging cradle doesn't just make your phone look more put together than a bunch of cables lying around. Instead, these cradles turn your phone into a device that can replace your clock radio, serve as a full-fledged stereo accessory, and direct you as an in-vehicle navigation system.

Using the desk cradle

The desk cradle, shown in Figure 16-15, is weighted and has a solid feel. The phone slides into the case in landscape orientation and connects to the mini-USB port on your phone to hold it in place.

Figure 16-15: The desk cradle for the Samsung Galaxy S.

Because each version of the Galaxy S is a little different, each has its own cradle. Be sure to order the correct cradle for your phone.

Depending upon the set-up of your house, you could use as many as three desk cradles, such as

- On your nightstand
- Next to your TV and stereo
- Next to your computer

The list price for this cradle is about $20, and you can purchase one at the retail store of your cellular carrier or online.

As you can see, the back has a port for the charging cable. This allows you to permanently plug the charging cable. An additional cable, which can be a nice convenience, has a list price of $20, but you can probably find one for as little as a few dollars.

On your nightstand

Your Samsung phone can serve as an alarm clock. In Chapter 8, I show you how to set alarms on your phone. By putting a desk cradle next to your bed, you can look at the screen right away.

By the way, the screen is usually dark before the alarm. When it's time to wake up, the phone turns on the screen by itself. You don't need to press the On button and unlock the screen to turn off that infernal alarm.

With your TV or stereo

In Chapter 13, I explore using your Samsung Galaxy S phone for entertainment. You can use your phone when you're mobile, but it can also plug in to your TV and/or stereo when it's set in its desk cradle. As shown in Figure 16-15, there's the port for a 3.5mm A/V cable that provides RCA jacks for your TV and/or your stereo.

When you want your phone to be a phone, you carry it with you. When you want it to be a stereo component, you slide it into your desk cradle that's pre-wired into your TV or stereo. With the USB power cable plugged in, you can watch the videos from V CAST or the Samsung Media Hub nonstop.

Some movies may not be licensed to run on your big screen TV. Before you invite all your friends over to watch a movie, you may want to verify that it will play.

When it's time to go out, just disconnect the phone and go.

Next to your computer

The USB outlets on your computer are a convenient way to charge your phone. You may also find it handy to keep your phone accessible when you are working hard (or playing hard or socializing hard) on your computer.

Responsibly relying on the car cradle

The car cradle, shown in Figure 16-16, has a suction cup that allows you to secure it to your dash or to your window. The phone slides into the cradle in either vertical or landscape orientation. There is also a connection on the back for the car charger that connects to the cigarette lighter/power adapter in your car.

Figure 16-16: The car cradle for the Samsung Galaxy S.

The car cradle costs about $35, and the car charger is another $15.

The Mapping applications that I discuss in Chapter 12 are that much more convenient to use when you have simplified access to the phone while you drive.

Follow the local rules about using a screen and a cellphone when driving. Please. Remember that I asked nicely.

Part VI
The Part of Tens

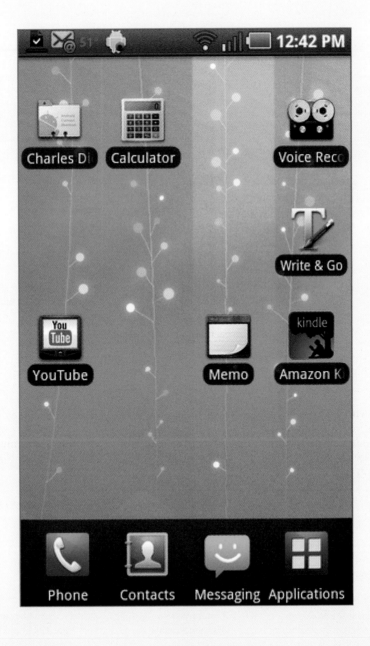

In this part . . .

The Part of Tens includes two chapters. Chapter 17 shows you how to customize your phone so it works exactly the way you want it to. In Chapter 18, I look at the ways Samsung can make the phone even better.

17

Ten (Or So) Ways to Make Your Phone Totally Yours

A cellphone is a very personal device. From the moment you take it out of the box and strip off the packaging, you begin to make it yours. By the end of the first day, even though millions of your type of phone may have been sold, there's no other phone just like yours.

This is the case not only because of the phone calls you make, but because of all the options that you can set on the phone and all the information that you can share over the Web. Your contacts, music files, downloaded videos, texts, and favorites make this phone a unique representation of who you are and what's important to you.

Even with all this "you" on your phone, this chapter covers ten-plus ways to further customize your phone beyond what I have already explored. I also explore one way that I suggest that you don't modify your phone!

Maximizing Shortcuts from Home

You won't spend much time there, but your extended Home screen is critical to your experience with your phone. Ideally, here are the shortcuts to the places you want to go most frequently with as little clutter as possible. This ideal is probably as likely as keeping your house immaculate day in and day out. Fortunately, keeping your Home screen clutter free is easier than cleaning up in the real world.

To keep Home as tidy and helpful as possible, remember that you can always do the following. Read more about how in Chapter 2.

✔ **Add shortcuts to the Home screen.**

- Contacts that you can quickly call or text
- Telephone numbers from contacts that you can tap and call
- Text addresses that allow you to tap and text
- Directions to a favorite place
- Folders where you've stored Microsoft Office files
- Apps or games that you use frequently; see Figure 17-1

Figure 17-1: Shortcuts I added to the extended Home screen to applications.

You can add shortcuts until the seven pages of your extended Home screen are full.

✔ **Remove shortcuts from the Home screen.**

You Look Mahvelous: Custom Screen Images

In addition to the shortcuts on your extended Home screen, you can also customize the images that are behind the screen. You can change the background to one of three options:

✔ Any picture from your Gallery can be virtually stretched across the seven screens of your home page. (Read more about Gallery in Chapter 10.)

✔ Choose a neutral background image (similar to the backgrounds on many PCs) from the wallpaper Gallery. Figure 17-2 is showing a background image.

✔ Opt for a "live" wallpaper that responds to touchscreen input.

Figure 17-2: A neutral background image.

The pictures from your Gallery and the Wallpaper Gallery are static images. After they're saved to your Home screen, they move only slightly as you scroll across your Home screens.

Personalizing Your App List

The next most important area for enjoying your phone is your Application list. Depending upon your phone, there are two options for personalizing this list:

✔ Switch between list view and grid view.

✔ Change the order of your applications.

Read how to make these changes in Chapter 8.

Adding Facebook to Your Contacts

You probably have a Facebook account. If you do, your Samsung Galaxy S can work with it in two ways:

- ✔ **Add a Facebook widget.** You can use this app to access the information on Facebook in a way that's comparable to what you do on a PC, but in a format more suitable for the screen size of your Galaxy S.

- ✔ **Integrate your Facebook with your contacts.** By syncing with your Facebook account, you automatically populate your contacts with your friends in your Facebook account. This includes their images.

Read how to do this in Chapter 5.

You can also add contacts from MySpace and Twitter.

Staying Current with Updates

After you add your social networks to your phone, you can track changes in them. From within Contacts, tap the Updates tab to see the latest news from your contacts that you added from Facebook, Twitter, or MySpace!

Playing Favorites with Some Contacts

All your contacts are important, but some are more important than others. Besides accessing a person's telephone number from their Contacts profile, here are some options you can use to dial them quickly:

- ✔ **Add the contact as a shortcut to your Home screen.** You can open the shortcut and then call, text, or e-mail that contact with a tap to that name and then a tap on the preferred communications method.

- ✔ **Add the contact's telephone number as a shortcut to your Home screen.** You can call her by tapping that name.

- ✔ **Make a given person in your Contacts a Favorite.** This puts that person on a special list on your Phone/Dialer page so that you can get to him faster. Figure 17-3 shows a contact that's designated a Favorite by the gold star next to his name.

Creating a Favorite is straightforward, as I explain in Chapter 5.

A Favorite contact

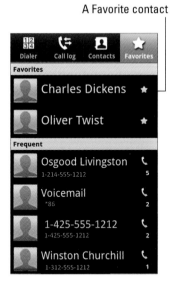

Figure 17-3: A favorite in your Contacts.

Making a Statement with Accessories

The Samsung Galaxy S is durable, but there are limits to how much abuse it can take. My advice: Get a wrapping (such as from Skinit, www.skinit.com) to protect your phone from scratches. Skins are more for appearance; cases do more for protection.

You can get cases from your cellular carrier and/or from Samsung. You can also get more of a selection or a lower price from a number of online retailers. These come in a variety of styles and materials. Just be sure that it fits your phone.

Getting Caught Up on Your Reading

You put music and videos on your phone. Why not put a good book on your phone as well? You can.

The service with the greatest selection of book titles for your Samsung Galaxy S is accessed through the Amazon Kindle app — which, depending upon your phone, might come preinstalled. If not, you can easily find it on Android Market. (Read all about Android Market in Chapter 9.)

When you open this app, you see the Home screen shown in Figure 17-4.

Figure 17-4: The Kindle app on your phone.

This screen shows the books you've downloaded, the place to get more books, and a link to get books you've already acquired, perhaps on another platform.

For some folks, e-books are a wonderful convenience. For others, the print is too hard to read. Because the app is free and many of the classics are free, though, try for yourself.

Securing Your Phone

When the phone goes into standby mode and the screen goes blank, depending upon the phone brand, you need to swipe your finger across the screen in some manner. Your phone will tell you what to do. For that matter, your phone will tell anyone who finds it how to get to your apps. At this point, anyone could use your phone and all the information stored on it.

To avoid this fate, I recommend putting security on your phone if you care at all about the information on your phone. Don't think you have anything on your phone that's very important? What about the names and addresses of everyone you know? Where you live? Your upcoming appointments (when you'll be away from home with an empty house just waiting to be looted)? Your financial information? All this kind of information is commonly found on people's cellphones, and if you lose your phone, a less-than-honorable person could wreak havoc with it.

Sure, having to get through a security option every time you want to use your phone is slightly inconvenient. But if you lose your phone, you'll be glad you have it. Read how to set security in Chapter 2.

Backing Up the Data on Your Phone

As a responsible user of a PC, I'm sure that you back up your data on a daily basis. That way, if your PC should have a catastrophic failure, you can easily rebuild your system without trouble. (Yeah, right.)

In practice, businesses are pretty good at the discipline of backing up PCs on corporate networks. However, the fact is that most of us are pretty lazy on our personal PCs. We back up our PCs only intermittently. I'd be surprised if you ever considered backing up your phone.

As I discuss in the last section, you'll likely have a great deal of valuable information on your phone. Maybe backing up your phone isn't such a bad idea in case you lose it or break it, or in case it's stolen or has a catastrophic failure.

Some cellular carriers, like Verizon, offer a backup service preinstalled on your phone: the Backup Assistant. You can access it from Accounts and Sync on your Settings page.

However, have no fear if your phone doesn't come preinstalled with such an application. Many services support Android phones in Android Market, and more are coming every day. In Chapter 9, read all about how to shop from the Market.

Rescuing a Lost Phone

Having your data backed up is a good thing, but I'm sure that you'd really rather just get your phone back if it's ever lost. There are apps available in the Android Market for practically any scenario. If you've lost or misplaced your phone, or if it's been stolen, you can rely on these features for help finding your cellular buddy:

✓ **Remote Ring:** By sending a text to your phone with the "right" code that you pre-programmed when you set up this service, your phone will ring on its loudest setting, even if you have the ringer set to Vibrate Only.

If you know that your phone is in your house, the accuracy of GPS isn't savvy enough to tell you whether it's lost between the seat cushions of your couch or in the pocket of your raincoat. That's where the Remote Ring feature comes in handy.

✔ **Map Current Location:** This feature allows you to track, within the accuracy of the GPS signal, the location of your phone. You need to access the Web site of the company with which you arranged to provide this service, and it will show you on a map the rough location of your phone.

If you have a friend that has you as a friend on Latitude, you can call them and get the same information. (Read all about Latitude in Chapter 12.)

✔ **Remote Lock:** This app allows you to create a four-digit pin (if you ignored the advice in the preceding section) that when sent to your phone from another cellular phone or a Web page, will lock down your phone. You can also have the Home screen display a message, such as, `If found, please call 212-555-1212`. Again, this app needs to be set up before your phone is stolen.

If you know that your phone was stolen — that is, not just lost — do *not* try to track down the thief yourself. Get the police involved and let them know that you have this service on your phone — and that you know where your phone is.

✔ **Remote Erase:** Also known as Remote Wipe, this option resets the phone to its factory settings, wiping out all the information and settings on your phone.

You can't add Remote Erase after you've lost your phone. You must sign up for premium service beforehand.

Each of the preceding kinds of applications are available from the Android Market. The simplest security applications are free, but the better quality apps are about $10 and require a monthly service fee in the range of up to $5 monthly.

Protecting against Malware

One of the main attractions for application developers to write apps for Android is that Google doesn't have a preapproval process for a new app to be placed on Android Market. This is unlike the Apple App Store or Microsoft Marketplace, where each derivation of an app is validated.

Many developers prefer to avoid the bureaucracy, but this does expose users like you and me to malware. Market forces, in the form of negative feedback, are present to kill apps, whether they are badly written or are meant to steal your private data. However, this works only after some poor soul has experienced problems — such as theft of personal information.

Rather than simply avoiding new apps, you can download apps to protect the information on your phone. These are available from many of the firms that make antivirus software for your PC. Importantly, many of these antivirus applications are free. If you want a nicer interface and some enhanced features, you can pay a few dollars, but this is not necessary.

Ten Features to Look for Down the Road

With the power of your Samsung Galaxy S and the flexibility offered in Android applications development, it can be difficult to imagine that there could be added capabilities not currently in the works. In spite of this, I have come up with ten features that would improve the usability and value of your Galaxy S phone.

Provide Folders for Web Bookmarks

Currently, bookmarks can be stored only in one long list. This might be a small annoyance, but some of us are very enthusiastic about storing Web pages.

Web browsers in your PC allow you to sort bookmarks into folders. You should be able to do this on your Galaxy S phone. Google, please make it so.

Side-loading Music, Videos, and Office Files

You can add files to your Galaxy S memory card by texting or e-mailing them as attachments. You can also load these files on your MicroSD card with a USB adapter — if you take the card out of your phone. It certainly would be nice to be able to connect the USB currently used for charging and transfer files.

Yeah, this isn't hard to implement technically. However, cellular carriers don't care much for this option because it bypasses their networks. Still, there needs to be a way to make this happen for the convenience of Galaxy S users.

Better Categorization for Videos

Right now, all videos — whether full-length movies, movie trailers, music videos, or camcorder files — are housed in one big folder. You can sort them by size, date, or name — not good enough. It's important to have more filing capability.

UMA on GSM Phones

The coverage of your cellular carrier is a critical issue for the enjoyment of your phone. The data services on your phone can work with Wi-Fi if the cellular data coverage is weak or gone. This isn't perfect, but it does allow your phone to be partially functional.

Some GSM-based phones support the Unlicensed Mobile Access (UMA) capability. This technology will switch a voice call to use Wi-Fi if you enter a place with good Wi-Fi coverage but no cellular coverage. It works seamlessly, and neither you nor the person on the other end of the call can tell that the call switched from one wireless option to another.

T-Mobile supports other UMA-capable phones, but UMA isn't on the T-Mobile Vibrant for some reason. AT&T Mobility doesn't currently support UMA, but it should consider using this technology.

Live Status Updates on Secure Screen

Whether you're using the default wake-up screen or you implemented the Unlock pattern (see Chapter 2), you need to unlock the phone screen to know whether you've received e-mails, texts, voicemails, or updates.

It would be a nice feature to present counts for the number of unopened e-mails, texts, and voicemails on the Secure screen.

Flexible Extended Home Screen

As I mention throughout this book, the extended Home screen is set to seven pages. I, as a user, should be able to control the size of this. If I want to make my extended Home screen smaller or larger, I should have that option.

Integration with Collaboration Tools

In Chapter 15, I discuss using the ThinkFree Office tools to work with Microsoft Office files. In that chapter, I point out that these are the bare minimum.

It would be a large improvement to integrate with the collaboration server tools that firms use to formally track revisions of documents. With the tools available right now, you need to personally keep track of which is the most current document. Collaboration tools do this automatically, however.

For the mass business market, Microsoft offers SharePoint server, and IBM has its Lotus Domino and Lotus Connection. There are dozens of other tools that serve particular niches. It would be very helpful to have my Galaxy S integrate with the services that this class of application provides.

External Keyboard and Screen

As I mention in the book, the Galaxy S phone is as powerful as a good laptop from a few years ago. The two capabilities that keep it from being a true laptop replacement are dictated by its size: The keyboard and screen are just too small for all-day use.

So, why not have an external keyboard and screen that are full size? The Redfly from Celio (`www.celiocorp.com`) is such a device, but it works only with Windows Phone Classic and the BlackBerry. It would be nice to have such an offering for the Galaxy S phone.

With a Redfly for your Galaxy S, your phone would be a phone when you're mobile. You would keep your Redfly in its case and just use the phone with its beautiful screen.

Then, when you need to do some serious work or want a full-sized screen, you connect your phone to the Redfly. Because the Redfly is only a screen and a keyboard, it's not too expensive and doesn't use a lot of power.

If Celio does not step up to serve the Galaxy S, others are pursuing this kind of solution. In fact, Motorola announced the Atrix 4G that has an optional laptop dock.

Supporting Mobile Device Management

In rough numbers, about two-thirds of all phones used in the United States are at least occasionally used for business purposes. Some are provided by a firm for its mobile employees. Some allow their employees to get their own phones. Of these, some employees get reimbursed, while others make business calls at their own expense.

Regardless of who pays, a large number of smartphone users are accessing corporate information: contacts or e-mail or super-secret files with financial forecasts.

Here's my point. After a company allows corporate information to go on to a phone, it has a responsibility to protect that information, no matter whose phone it is.

This is one of the functions of a class of applications called Mobile Device Management (MDM). Good MDM software knows who has downloaded what information to what device and what level of security is turned on and set properly for this phone, if any.

Currently, implementation of MDM applications is spotty at best. At the same time, many states have implemented severe penalties if a company doesn't protect customer data. With the 32GB MicroSD cards that are available, an employee could walk around with the name, credit card number, Social Security number, and other personal data of every customer on his belt.

Fortunately, this hasn't happened . . . yet. MDM, along with other company policies, can help address this threat from becoming a nightmare scenario.

Safer Rooting

Some users have found it useful to "jailbreak" their phone to get root access in an effort to enable applications that do more. There should be an official way for users who want these advanced capabilities to get there without also risking messing up important settings.

Index